Pr(

"The story of *Starchild* is extraordinary in every way: heart-breaking, profound, personal, brave, hopeful and deeply inspiring."
— Helen Sedgwick, author of *The Comet Seekers* and *The Growing Season*

"I loved this book from start to finish. The journey Marsh takes from the death of her adopted brother to searching for his family in Uganda hits hard on so many emotional levels. It reminds us of the resiliency of the human spirit and what can be accomplished when one is fueled by conviction. *Starchild* is both a love story to a brother taken too soon and a bright spotlight directed onto the challenges of foster care and adoption."
— Charles de Lint, author of *Moonheart* and *The Wind in His Heart*

"*Starchild* is an odyssey; a spiritual voyage of self-discovery. Michaela Foster Marsh, through sheer – obsessive even – dedication, illuminates and highlights a path, no matter how jaggedly rocky, that can help lead towards emotional fulfillment."
— Peter McDougal, BAFTA and Prix Italia award-winning screenwriter

"Wow! I knew Michaela Foster Marsh was a fantastic singer. I didn't know she was also a fantastic writer. Her book about her brother Frankie and the ever-twisting route that took her to changing the lives of children in Uganda is part detective novel, part intense soul-searching about the realities of adoption, and part travelogue about the colorful, and sometimes scary, reality of dealing with elusive individuals and organizations in Africa. What Michaela and her partner Rony achieved in Uganda is astonishing. The fact she can describe it so movingly in the written word is equally breathtaking."
— Ken Smith, Columnist, *The Herald*

Starchild

Starchild

A Memoir of Adoption, Race, and Family

Michaela Foster Marsh

Author note: I have tried to recreate events, locales and conversations from my memories of them. In order to maintain their anonymity in some instances, I have changed the names of individuals. I may have changed some identifying characteristics and details such as physical properties.

The Story Plant
Studio Digital CT, LLC
PO Box 4331
Stamford, CT 06907

Story Plant Trade Paperback ISBN-13: 978-1-61188-301-5
Story Plant Hardcover ISBN-13: 978-1-61188-275-9
Fiction Studio Books E-book ISBN-13: 978-1-945839-38-2

Visit our website at www.thestoryplant.com

First Story Plant Hardcover Printing: April 2020
First Story Plant Trade Paperback Printing: April 2021
Printed in the United States of America

This book is dedicated to my brother
Frankie Marsh

Introduction

It's Christmas, 1993. I'm unexpectedly offered a paid three-week vacation back home to Scotland over the holidays. Considering I'm living in Ottawa, Canada and haven't been home in three years, I don't hesitate. I can't believe my luck and neither can my family.

My brother Frankie and I often went out together in Glasgow in our late teens and early twenties. Being home for the Christmas holidays is a real reason to celebrate. A lot of new bars and clubs have opened in Glasgow since I've been away and Frankie seems hell-bent on his sister seeing them all. But there is one night in particular I will never forget.

We're sitting together at a round metal table. The new bar's busy and noisy. Frankie has a beer in his hand. I have a vodka and coke. He starts singing along to the song playing in the background. It's a jazz funk song and he moves along to the funky beat of the music as he always does, laughing his infectious laugh. Suddenly he stops singing and looks at me with half-glazed eyes, shouting above the music, "If anything ever happens to me, I want this song played at my funeral. It's brilliant. The lyrics are just amazing."

I laugh. "Don't be ridiculous. That's just the drink talking."

"Just promise me, if anything ever happens, you'll play this song. It's called 'Starchild' by Level 42."

"Yeah, okay but you're drunk. Nothing's going to happen to you."

"I know, but just in case." He raises his beer to me. "Cheers on it."

We clink glasses and he smiles one of his big huge smiles, his white teeth flashing against his black African skin.

Just over six weeks later, on February 26, 1994, my adopted Ugandan brother Frankie died in an accidental fire in his flat in Glasgow. He was twenty-seven years old.

Starchild

When I was an infant in my mother's arms
I would watch the starlight in her face
'Cause I was reaching out to understand the cosmic charm
I am just a Starchild born in space

Way up high above the sky, all that beauty passes by
Whole worlds still unknown
And out beyond the blue, there's a place for people too
It's time for us to go

I have seen the sun shine bright in paradise
I have been there, I have seen it
Everywhere space people stare through ageless eyes
I have seen them, I believe it

Way up high above the sky, all that beauty passes by
Whole worlds still unknown
And out beyond the blue, there's a place for people too

Starchild

It's time for us to go
We have time
(in my dreams)
Time and space
while we're young
(floating free)
We can chase to the stars

Searching for the magic in the universe
Guided by the stars that light my way
I have seen the sun shine bright in paradise
I am just a Starchild born in space
If you want to go with me I'll take you there
I've been shown these secrets face to face
I have seen the sun shine bright in paradise
I am just a Starchild born in space

This book is about the remarkable journey of finding my adopted brother's family in Uganda, eighteen years after his death, and how I discovered the magic in the universe. The unexpected twists and turns and remarkable coincidences that happened to me were deeply emotional and magical. On this soul-searching journey, I discovered as much about myself as I did my brother's family.

I know now that there is a continuous thread that connects us, even after death. Loss in life is real, as is the agony that follows that loss. Everyone has a story. Our lives are shaped by where and who we come from. In life, there can be massive successes, failures, losses, heartaches, loves and deaths. The draw is unique to each person, as is how they respond and the ways in which they have to find within themselves their resilience and sheer determination to survive. I've learned self-pity is perhaps the worst enemy in life. It doesn't matter where in the world you come from, or how privileged or oppressed you are, this journey showed me that life is about strength of spirit and the remarkable ability to heal, transform and transcend. I believe, if we ask, help is sent, but it is in response to our actions and faith that we are being listened to. I have come to appreciate the invisible world within me and around me— to appreciate my blessings and the divine cosmic nudges that are always present. I have learned the smallest act of kindness can never be underestimated for the person giving and the person receiving, and it has the power to resonate long after a person has gone.

CHAPTER ONE
Uganda Time

Gayaza High School,
Gayaza, Wakiso District,
Buganda Region,
Uganda, 2012

I'm here. I'm actually here, in Uganda, standing outside the gates of Gayaza High School for Girls. I cannot *wait* to get past this daunting checkpoint and through these iron gates.

The sentry box at the checkpoint is vacant. I peer through the large metal gates. The tree-lined path to the main grounds of the school is massive. Old colonial-style buildings sit strategically on manicured lawns. If it wasn't for the heat and the cricket noises, I might think I'm waiting to enter a convent in rural England. The sign ahead that reads *No Boy Contact* reinforces my unease. It's not hard to imagine a Mother Superior, rod in hand, patrolling the girl's dormitories. However, the only person patrolling the grounds today is the security guard I've spied having a smoke under one of the many trees, which are unfamiliar to me.

A shamba boy lazily sweeps the dry dust and leaves from the path ahead. Bent almost double, his short broom makes me think he could make his job last all day. The rhythmic sound of the sweeping makes everything seem like it's in slow motion. But I'm in a hurry—I want to burst through these locked gates! I've traveled over four thousand miles to be here. I've had sixteen injections, including yellow fever, dengue fever, typhoid, rabies, diphtheria, cholera, meningococcal meningitis, hepatitis A, B and C, and I'm downing antimalarials every day. However, in the past few weeks since arriving in Uganda, I have learned there is something called "Uganda time." It means anytime. No one is in a hurry here, except the small lizard that has just scurried across the path in front of me. I jump back and a large flock of birds descend noisily on a nearby tree, squabbling over which branch to take up residence in. I yelp and slap my mosquito-repellent-clammy skin before some insect takes residence on me!

The security guard finally notices my partner Rony and me. Rony wouldn't let me come to Uganda on my own and has decided to take on the role of the "bodyguard." The fact that Rony looks like Arsène Wenger, the football manager of Arsenal, has meant that frankly, it's Rony who needs a "bodyguard"—not me. Everyone wants to shake his hand and try out for his football club.

The security guards stubs out his cigarette on the grass. Today we have a meeting arranged with the head teacher. Oh, God, I'm nervous enough. I have a fear of head teachers. Mrs. Edminston, one of my long-standing primary school teachers managed to instill that fear. She made our head teacher sound like a woman who sat in a den at the back of the school waiting to morph into some four-legged, fire-breathing dragon whenever Mrs. Edminston brought her a child *she* deemed to be stupid—usually me. However, her idle threats of sending me to see the head teacher never made me spell any better. They only gave me nightmares about what this dragon would do to me if I *was* sent to her "den." But now, this angry-looking guard is coming toward me with his rifle.

Potholes and Pitfalls

Nothing can prepare a visitor for the assault on the senses that is Uganda. It has exceptional wealth and exceptional poverty, exceptional beauty and exceptional unattractiveness. It can appear to lack visual sophistication, but look further and you will glimpse the magnificence in the meager and the brilliance in the broken. It is a country of vast natural resources and human potential. I cannot begin to explore the extreme contrasts of Uganda in this book alone. Neither am I an expert on this massively diverse country. But the rich, varied, and unexpected experiences one can have in Uganda bear witness to Uganda's unique culture and history.

Uganda is often mistaken as having been a colony of the United Kingdom but was, in fact, a Protectorate of the United Kingdom. Although it gained independence in 1962 it had already absorbed many aspects of old British colonialism, many of which are still superimposed onto its own culture. It is debatable whether this is for good or ill.

Some parts of Uganda are still resistant to change in both the social and religious sectors, and have remained unchanged for centuries. Attempts to destroy or change some tribal cultures have proved too great a challenge; the tribal culture is too ingrained. In some villages, life remains much the same today as it was thousands of years ago. The fast-paced modern city of Kampala appears to have fully embraced westernization. However, scratch the surface and underneath the age-old mythologies, loyalties and obligations still rule. The only difference is that nowadays Christianity seems to be inextricably linked with every aspect of life.

Uganda is not for the faint of heart. You could lose your car in the potholes and your life savings in some of its everyday pitfalls. Learning to adapt to its bedlam is a necessity. Resist it and you might as well retreat to what will, on return, seem an overwhelmingly dull home. It's best to embrace Uganda with every fiber of your body. If you're anything like me, your tummy will be the first bit of your anatomy to let you know you are out of your comfort zone. And no amount of mosquito repellent and nets will repel those nasty little insects. I remember watching the Dalai Lama on television being asked about the Buddhism doctrine on all creatures having a right to live. He said he agreed, but that he had a real problem with mosquitoes. He pretended one was on his arm, sucking his blood; he looked at it with real compassion then smacked his hand on the imaginary insect and exclaimed, "Nazi!" I can relate.

And guidebooks simply *cannot* be trusted! A restaurant in Kampala got five stars, maybe for the performance of the twenty-five plus rats that were running in and out of the ovens and work tops of the open-plan kitchen! Sadly we did not catch sight of these performing rats till *after* we had eaten there. I remember Rony grabbing his camera to photograph them. I thought the proprietor was going to stop him but he moved to put more lights on so Rony could get a better shot. The worrying thing, over and above having just eaten our meals, was that the owner didn't see anything wrong with the safari in his kitchen. I finally decided we really had to leave when Rony started suggesting to the proprietor that he could increase his turnover by opening a shooting gallery and supplying his guests with air rifles.

However, the dichotomy of the country is also evident in the food establishments. There are a number of exceptionally fine restaurants in Uganda; in fact, some are amongst the best I've eaten in. And, accommodation is as diverse as its people. Still, if you are thinking of going to Uganda, pack a sense of humor—you'll need it!

Nothing compares to Ugandan society and with the right attitude you can not only survive the chaos but also learn that life is not a right but rather an honor. The things we take for granted are privileges known by few in this diverse and complex planet we inhabit.

I reckon it goes against most people's nature to distrust, but when it comes to Uganda I had to teach myself to reverse that instinct until a person proved otherwise. It's sad but true; corruption is ruining the country. Lying, cheating and stealing have become part of daily life. Ugandan's call it "Financial Engineering." I soon discovered that just because someone seems *very* nice and tells me they are a Christian does not mean they are above deceiving me. Of course, trust has to work both ways. It's always important to give relationships time and to be vigilant. Everyone has a sad story to tell, and if you are anything like me then they can suck you in quicker than you can let out the breath you've been holding while listening to their tragedy. History tells Ugandans that we muzungus are very wealthy; therefore, the opportunist is never far from your side. They come in all disguises—even church collars.

I am not saying any of this out of any prejudice. Some of the most beautiful people I know are Ugandan. They are amongst the warmest, friendliest people anyone might ever meet. And it is hard not to be moved by some of their personal daily struggles and desire to overcome the nightmares of the past, especially when you know Uganda's history. The country's natural beauty and its warm-hearted people belie the horror of its dark past. (But I know only too well some of the pitfalls for the wide-eyed, do-good traveler, charitable bodies and potential adoptive parents.)

The country has always attracted its fair share of "white saviors." Many I have frankly found somewhat reckless and distasteful. Some, I feel use Uganda as a bit of a playground. Thankfully, most don't seem to last long. However, some have created havoc and then, when things haven't worked out *their* way, left. I'm sure most, like me, started with good intentions but what can feel like the best thing to do isn't always *the* best. Sadly, our white muzungu ignorance can sometimes end up making things worse. Just as the misconceptions and assumptions Ugandan's have about white people can cause problems too. But, I have also witnessed some incredible initiatives and projects that have been carefully developed by the muzungus. And, thank God for them.

Dad and Frankie the day he was adopted

18

Family Secrets

Scotland, 1976

I'm sitting at the kitchen dinner table, swinging my legs under the seat that is too big for me. Mum is working and Dad has cooked us dinner: cheesy scrambled eggs—what Dad *always* cooks when Mum is working.

"Dad, someone called Frankie and me bad words today."

"Oh, really. And what were those words?"

I look down at my dinner plate and play with my food.

"It's okay," Dad reassures me. "You can tell me."

"They called Frankie a *black bastard* and me a *nigger lover.*"

"Oh, really. And what did you call them?"

"Nothing. We just ignored them."

"Well, I wish I could say the same about the young boy who called me a bastard at school. I think I left his face rather deformed."

Frankie looks up from his plate. "Why would anyone call you a *bastard*?" I can tell Frankie's enjoying the freedom of being able to use a bad word.

"Because, my dear children, I didn't know who my father was either."

I stop eating and look at Dad. "What do you mean? Grandpa's your dad."

"Yes. But he's my adopted dad."

Frankie swallows his food. "You mean you're *adopted* too, like me?"

"Yes, I am."

"I don't understand, Dad. Why did no one tell us? That means Granny and Grandpa Marsh aren't *really* our grandparents."

"Of course they are. That's like saying we're not really Frankie's parents."

"No. I don't mean that. I know they're your parents but who are your *real* parents?"

"To be honest sweetheart, I'm not sure who my dad is, but maybe your aunt Sissy could answer that."

"Aunt Sissy. Why would Aunt Sissy know?"

"Because she's my *real* mum."

Frankie and I both look at each other, eyes wide open. Mouths agape.

Aunt Sissy is my favorite. Everyone tells me I take after her because I can sew. I make all my own dolls' dresses. I even make tops for myself and soft toys. I'm good at those. But Aunt Sissy can make *anything*. She makes all her own clothes. She's even made me a long skirt with fancy gold buttons which I *love*. I'm thinking, *if she's Dad's real mum, that must be why I can sew so well. But surely Aunt Sissy wouldn't have given up my dad.*

Frankie laughs. "You're joking us now, Dad." He rocks back and forth on his chair.

"No. I'm not joking son. Your aunt Sissy is my mum."

"Wow. Really?" Frankie is still rocking back and forth in his chair—with even more enthusiasm. He's enjoying this story much more than I am.

I feel confused. I need to ask more questions. "So, that must mean that Uncle John is your dad?"

"No. I told you, I don't know who my dad is and to be honest, I don't much care to know. As far as I'm concerned, Gran and Grandpa Marsh adopted me and they are my *real* parents."

Frankie shrugs his shoulder as if to say *fine* and carries on eating. I'm confused as to why he seems to be taking this so well, and I'm feeling distressed. I like my aunt Sissy. This doesn't add up. "I don't understand,

Dad. If Aunt Sissy is your mum, why did Gran have to adopt you?"

"I'm not sure sweetheart, but I guess Aunt Sissy had her reasons for not wanting me."

I feel tears welling up. How could she not have *wanted* my dad? My dad is the most amazing dad in the world. Until a few minutes ago, I thought Aunt Sissy was amazing too but she gave up my dad. Why? What would make her do such a thing to *my* dad?

Frankie asks, "Did you do something bad, Dad?"

"No, I didn't. Just like you didn't do anything bad either. I wasn't born and your aunt Sissy had already decided she didn't want me. That's why your Gran and Grandpa stepped in and adopted me. I was brought up to believe your aunt Sissy was my sister, until I was about fourteen years old."

"How'd you find out?" Frankie asks.

Dad pours himself another cup of tea. "Well, I was on my way for my first job interview and my well-meaning *brother* told me the truth...just in case the employer asked why I had the same name as him. That's when I discovered that Willie wasn't my brother. He was actually my uncle."

Frankie nods, fork in hand. "How'd you feel when he told you?"

"It was a bit of a blow but I always knew something wasn't right—that there was a secret surrounding me. Suddenly things started to add up."

I start sniffing. I'm not sure if I'm upset for Dad or myself, but I think both. There is a crack in my family that I wasn't aware of ten minutes ago. I thought I took after my aunt Sissy but right now, I don't understand her giving up my dad. I don't think I take after her at all. We might both like to sew but that's it! That is where the similarity ends. She hurt Dad. My ten-year-old sensitivities are strong. In fact, it all adds up now. All those times she was drunk and started cuddling Dad and calling him son. Dad always seemed annoyed when she did that and like a fly bothering him, he'd shoo her away. Now I know why. I always wondered about that. Why did I never ask?

Dad puts his arms around me. "Aw twinkle toes. Don't be sad sweetheart. I know it's a lot to take in, but loads of people have family secrets. I'm glad this isn't a secret anymore and you both know the truth. Besides, I kind of like the idea that I don't know who my dad is; I can imagine him as *anything* I want. That helps me imagine I can be anything I want to be...including a great singer!"

Dad starts singing *Scarlet Ribbons* to me. Then he stands up and puts on his comical thespian delivery. "You know my young fledglings, mythology abounds with adopted children. One of the most famous adoptions was Moses—the Ten Commandments were received from God by an adopted child. In Roman law, the royal bastard was even given special privileges, and England's first Norman king was openly known as *William the Bastard.*"

Frankie laughs. "William—that's your name!"

"Hey," I pipe up having just seen Star Wars. "Luke Skywalker was adopted, too, and he didn't know who his real dad was either."

"Indeed," says Dad. "And there are many fine examples of the historical, social status of the adopted child. And scores of world achievers and leaders have been adopted or spent their lives as orphans. So if anyone ever calls you a bastard again, Frankie, and you feel like punching them, you'll be able to give them a history lesson along with your left hook."

With that, Dad takes to his feet and starts shadow boxing. He loves prancing around, pretending to still be in the boxing ring of his youth. It makes us laugh, especially as he gets Frankie up on his feet and shows him a few bobs and weaves.

Later that evening Dad calls us both to the living room. He has a manila folder in front of him. Dad says that perhaps we would like a wee chat about Frankie's adoption and his African parents.

It feels a bit like I'm getting ready to hear a fairy tale. We're going to find out who Frankie's *real* African parents are! I mean, there was never any point in anyone trying to hide the fact that Frankie was adopted.

One time, when we were in the bathtub, Frankie said to Mum, "If I scrub really hard Mum, will I become white like Michaela?"

Quick as a flash, Mum said, "No, because you have special skin. You have *African* skin."

Just the way she said *African* made it sound exciting to me. I knew my parents had never been to Africa because Frankie was born here.

"But *why* have I got a different skin color?"

"Well, as you know, your first parents came from an exotic country far, far away and it's very hot there. Because your skin is dark it is protected from the sun. Not like Michaela; we have to cover her in sunscreen lotion when the sun is out, otherwise she burns. And the sun brings out all her freckles, doesn't it, Michaela?"

"I hate my freckles! I wish I could scrub away my freckles."

"I've told you before that freckles are a sign of beauty. You'll both wish your life away. God made you who you are and you're both special and unique. The only thing you both need to scrub away is the dirt—especially behind your ears."

But now Dad is opening the folder.

Frankie's mum and dad might be some kind of African princess and prince. I'd seen *that* kind of stuff on

TV with all those fancy costumes and headpieces. *This is exciting! Maybe we'll go to Africa together! But they'd better not want him back. Oh, no...he'd better not want to go back. Oh, no...what if he wants to go meet them? Better not go there...keep that folder shut, Dad! I want to keep my brother! I love my brother! No one is taking him away from me!*

"I am sorry to say we really don't have very much information to go on."

I suddenly feel relief. I look at Frankie; his right knee is shaking up and down, the way it always does when he's anxious.

Dad looks at Frankie too, "I'm sorry Mum's not here tonight, but I think now might be a good time to at least share with you the information we have about your birth parents and the days before you came to live with us."

Frankie's looking down; knee going like a jackhammer. Dad says, "You know Mum and I love you very much. We just don't want you to feel we know any more than you do about your African parents or that we're holding on to some big secret."

Frankie lifts his head. He is close to tears. "But *you're* my parents. I don't want to know anything about my other parents. They didn't want to know me, and I don't want to know them! I don't want to know anything about Africa either! I'm Scottish!"

No one would deny it. He loves his Rangers football team. He speaks with a strong Glaswegian accent and is proud to wear the kilt.

Dad calmly closes the folder and pushes it aside. "A day might come when you change your mind. Just know that if you *ever* want to know anything, anything at all, it will not change the way your Mum and I feel about you. We love you and always will. I promise we'll do our best to help you trace any information. The information we have right now is limited, that's the way adoption was when you were born, but it's in here, in this folder. It's here for you, if and when you're ready."

As it turned out, Frankie wasn't ready until just months before he died.

Pandora's Box

Scotland, 2009

There is a lot to be said for not opening Pandora's Box. But I was always a curious child and, by the age of forty-three, I was *still* just as curious.

After both my parents died, that same manila folder loomed large with its penciled heading, *Frankie's Adoption*. It sat in a pile of paperwork I had inherited. As a child, I had often wondered about the information it contained and, probably like Frankie must have done, imagined who his parents were and the circumstances surrounding his adoption. Were they villains or heroes?

All through childhood it had been Frankie's decision to open or not open that folder. Now it was mine. I can only say I was as curious and apprehensive to open that folder as if it had been my own parents I was about to find out about.

I hate secrets. They're like shadows over everything. Maybe it goes back to the family secret of Aunt Sissy. The fact that my brother's life had this adoption secrecy surrounding it since childhood bothered me.

By the size and weight of the folder I knew I would be lucky to find five pages in there, and for all I knew it could be social work jargon. But this was the folder Dad had offered Frankie all those years ago, so there was a good chance that at least *some* information about his parents was still in there.

I wanted an ending to the endless stories I had created about his parents. But deep down I knew I wouldn't get an ending. What I would most likely get is another story. But what if I didn't like the *real* story? Wouldn't it be easier to keep my fairy tales and keep that folder shut? The truth can often hurt.

I sat looking at the thin, musty folder, wondering if his parents' names could be in there. To even know their names would be fantastic. A name could tell me so much, but what was I thinking, an African name wouldn't give me *any* background clues—at all. It wouldn't be like discovering my grandfather was a MacDonald and all the clan history that went along with that and the all-important difference between McDonald and MacDonald. I remember my mum telling me someone gave my grandfather a check with the name McDonald on it and he wouldn't cash it. It was an abomination to call him a McDonald.

I suspected Frankie's parents had most likely lived through turbulent times. What if there were some gruesome details lurking inside this folder? Frankie was a branch from an ancestral tree that got cut off and blown into the wind. Far off in a distant land he was disconnected from his roots, yet the memory of all who had gone before must have somehow been contained in my brother. I had developed a curiosity about the trauma of our ancestors, their spiritual and emotional legacies and how much of that affects us. I knew I was unlikely to garner that kind of information in this small folder but I was frightened that I might discover something sinister about his parents. I also knew they could have done *anything*, and it wouldn't have changed my love for Frankie.

I wanted his mother to have wanted him. I wanted the circumstances to be such that she couldn't keep him. That was the story I had created. Well, it was the story my parents told us. Titbits of sugar-coated information got mentioned from time to time, and I feasted on them. However, I was never sure if it was the truth or if my parents were trying to make it easier for Frankie. What if I discovered otherwise? What if she hadn't wanted him? I believed the hurt would be as painful as if it had been my painful rejection. The reality was I could be left grieving a false tale. But it felt as though something supernal wanted me to uncover these childhood secrets and find Frankie's roots. It was almost as if I, too, was disconnected from those roots. And so, forty-three years after Frankie's adoption, I decided to open the manila folder.

On top of the contents, I discovered a letter from Dad to Frankie. Dad photocopied everything he ever sent to anyone. This was before email and computers and Dad always said it was safer to have a copy of any correspondence with *everyone*. From the date of the letter, Frankie would have been about twenty-six years old. What I discovered from reading it was that Frankie, who was living in London at that time, was now curious about his birth parents and had wondered if Dad could give him any information. That frightening curiosity and emptiness had finally gotten the better of him.

Frankie had moved back to Glasgow shortly after the letter was written, and died tragically in a fire in his flat. The original documents were all still in the manila envelope. I wept.

He had left this earth with a gaping hole in his heart—a void he had not been able to fill. He had an ever-present ghost of parents he was part of, yet wasn't. Oh, how I wanted to talk to him and ask if he was at peace now. Had his spirit been able to fly to Uganda and find his mother? Or was he where I imagined him, in her arms on the other side of a thin veil where life still goes on.

What a waste of years, I thought. He could have done what I was doing now! What took him so long to ask to see that folder? Had he been afraid of hurting our parents or had he been afraid of finding out the truth? Would finding his family have helped him understand the amalgam that he was? Would it have taken away his fears, his sense of being alone in the world, even when he wasn't? He had us. But it wasn't enough. We all knew that.

I wondered if it was just as well he hadn't found out any information and gone on some pilgrimage to find his family. Maybe it would have led to disappointment and hurt. He might have looked African, but he was Scottish. But perhaps he had been deliberately or unconsciously in love with Scotland out of loyalty...or was it fear? I remember a distinct uneasiness when people would ask him where he was from and his slightly defensive response, "What do you mean? I'm from here. I'm Scottish." Could he have really found a sense of belonging in Africa that he couldn't here? I doubted it, but I understood his longing to know, for I did too.

The next page in the folder read:

> *Francis Kaggwa Wevugira.*
> *Born 22/9/66 at 9.35am at Thornhill Hospital.*
>
> *Mother: Janet Wevugira. 28 Yrs of age. Student Teacher, having trained in Uganda and Belfast. Her father was a Minister in Uganda. Four sisters and five brothers, cousin a Doctor in Belfast. Height 5'3'. Dark skin.*

P.F. (putative father) Gedion Kaggwa. 30 Yrs of age. Student Doctor from Uganda. Height 5' 8'. Dark skin. One sister. Said he went to U.S.A. prior to the placement.

Janet Wevugira. The name rolled around in my head and then my tongue. It was like eating a sweetie. Janet Wevugira. I said it out loud as best I could, trying to get the pronunciation. *So, you were my brother's mother.* I began to wonder what this small woman named Janet looked like. I wondered about everything to do with this woman; I had always wondered. In my imagination, she had been about 5'5", shapely, exotic, and beautiful. She was warm, affectionate and had this huge smile—just like Frankie. I had always thought she had been around twenty years old when she had given birth to him, and she had stayed that age. I never thought of her as aging. But I did think about her at some of his birthdays and wondered if she quietly thought about him from Uganda. But was she even in Uganda? I remember that, sometimes if an African woman got on a bus or was walking down the street near us, I would wonder if perhaps that was Frankie's mum. Maybe she never went back to Uganda. Perhaps that titbit of information about her having to return to Uganda was to protect him or even her? I never vocalized these thoughts about her—not even to Frankie. But then Frankie always seemed oddly incurious. I think I knew better than to go there and so my bright imagination was left in the dark to gather dust—just like this folder.

I read on through the letter headed from The Church of Scotland Committee on Social Responsibility.

2nd April 1968

Little Francis had been placed directly into the Tanker Ha' Children's Home on the 30th September. Francis' mother and father are from Uganda. They were both students in this country; she, as a student teacher and he, a medical student. The mother wished to keep Francis and hoped to take him home to Uganda after her studies. The father, however, would not marry her and he left for the United States, insisting upon his son's adoption. The mother returned to Uganda after her final examinations and decided it was impossible for her to take the child there without being married to the father. Pre-marital pregnancy would be totally unacceptable and, in addition, she feared for the effect this would have on the health of her father, a Minister of the Church of Uganda and an elderly man.

Poor Janet, I thought to myself. She really *had* wanted to keep Frankie. I knew it! I couldn't imagine how she must have felt giving up her baby like that. She never got to know her own son, my brother. And the father! Getting her pregnant and then leaving her alone in a foreign country to have her baby and hide away in shame. Was she on her own? How lonely she must have been. Did she ever get over that loss?

I started to think about Janet more and more, visualizing her and the pain she must have felt giving up her child. As the months went on I became ever more anxious to know who this Janet Wevugira was. Did she marry? Did she have any other family? Could I have brothers and sisters out there in Africa? But they wouldn't *really* be *my* brothers or sisters! There seemed to be more missing from the jigsaw puzzle now that I knew her name and had read a bit about her. It felt like I really *had* opened a Pandora's Box.

I started to search the internet, but there were very few leads. Wevugira turned out to be a very unusual name. I found one Wevugira in Uganda on Facebook. I contacted him but never mentioned the full connection to protect Janet. I just said she had been in the UK at one point, we had lost touch and I wondered, if he was, by chance, a relation. It turned out he was no relation. However, he was very anxious to try to find Janet for me and I quickly realized it would come at a cost. Once I started to get a daily onslaught of his impoverished relatives and friends, I knew I had to block him. At that point, Rony was concerned I could be opening myself up to exploitation as I had no idea who or what I could be dealing with on the internet. Rony felt that someone could fabricate a story about Janet in order to extricate money from me and give me false hope. He was right, of course, and so I gave up my internet search for "family" connections.

I did however manage to find Tanker Ha' Children's Home in Kilmarnock on the internet. I discovered it had been closed in 2008 and had been subdivided into six modern flats. Regardless, I wanted to see where Frankie had spent his first thirteen months of life, and so Rony and I took the twenty-mile drive toward the coast. I was so excited to see it!

Finally, there it was—the place my brother had spent his first thirteen months of life. The place my parents first laid eyes on him was in this beautiful old Victorian mansion occupying a corner of London Road. I stood outside and thought about him as a tiny baby being taken from his mum to live in this children's home—to live in a room crammed with cribs. I felt such pain for those abandoned souls who could not nurse on their mothers' breasts nor feel their mothers' heartbeat. The sheer terror of being so small and vulnerable to the mercy of strangers for your every need...God, I hoped they had been kind.

I imagined my parents seeing my brother for the first time, the mix of emotions they must have felt and the hard decision they made to adopt a black child into a white family in the '60s. I imagined the fears they must have had and their dreams for him, for our family. And of course, I thought about Janet. Did she know where her son had been placed when he was taken from her arms in Thornhill Hospital? I thought about the distance that was now between them. I felt I wanted to find her and reassure her that he had been adopted by a good family.

There was no birth certificate in the files. I became fixated on getting a proper birth certificate for Frankie; he had a death certificate but not a birth certificate. I was told by the authorities that adopted people weren't allowed to have their full birth certificates—only extracts—but I just wanted to have one for him, for me. A birth certificate would bring me closer to Janet, to his birth. It would also hopefully give me an address for Janet at the time of birth.

I knew from the papers on Frankie's adoption that Janet had been studying in Belfast. However, according to another letter in the manila folder from the Church of Scotland, Committee on Social Responsibility, Frankie's birth had been registered in Johnstone, Paisley, just outside Glasgow, in Scotland. How on earth did Janet get herself from Belfast to Scotland? And why? Was she pregnant when she made the journey? Did anyone help her or did she make the journey alone in secrecy?

I called the Johnstone Registry office in Paisley, and a lady answered. I explained that I was looking for my adopted brother's birth certificate.

"I'm afraid that I can't give you a birth certificate for an adopted person."

"But he died in 1994. He's not going to look for his parents. I just want to have one for him."

"I'm very sorry to hear that but I still can't give it to you."

I was so disappointed and it must have shown in my voice. I told her I had all the details from his adoption papers. Without waiting on her answer, I fired off the entry date, the entry number, district, year and the office the entry was made.

There was a long silence.

I broke it, "I know the mother's name."

"What's the mother's name?"

"Janet Wevugira. He was born in Thornhill Hospital."

"What is it you are looking for my dear? You seem to have all the information I have here."

"Oh, wow, so you have it. You have it in front of you!"

"Yes," she chuckled, "I can see it here."

"Do you know where his mum lived?"

"You tell me."

"Somewhere ...here in ...Glasgow." I said it with some uncertainty.

"I think you mean Belfast."

"Oh yes! She was a student there. That's in the adoption papers. But I thought she must have moved here as she had him in Paisley."

Luckily for me, this lady agreed to send me his birth certificate—well it was an extract, but it had all the information I needed! I will never know what made her agree to send it to me, but I was so excited. Thank you—whoever you were!

Until I received the registration in the post, I didn't have an address for Janet's residence. As it turned out, at the time of her pregnancy she was staying at Queen Mary's Hostel, 70 Fitzwilliam Street, Belfast. I felt a need to see where Janet had been living when Frankie was conceived. I decided to book a flight as soon as I could, hoping for more clues about Janet and my brother's origins.

The City that Launched a Thousand Dreams

Belfast, 2011

As I strolled along the dull pavements of Belfast, I was accompanied by the endless loop of the tune from the old tearjerker movie *Born Free*. I hadn't seen it since I was a child, the vast golden plains of Africa set against a backdrop of blue skies and burning orange suns. My head filled with romanticized notions of where Janet came from, a land of lions lounging around in the heat and flocks of birds rising and landing on acacia trees in the African bush. The world of *Born Free* was so far removed from Belfast that I struggled to imagine how Janet must have felt when she came to this strange land of gray buildings and divided people.

I started to imagine Janet trying to understand that strange Northern Irish accent. I could hardly decipher it myself. And the weather—I know Uganda has its rainy season, but I wondered if Belfast had any other season? It was as wet as Glasgow. But it wasn't just the weather; the people seemed to be almost exclusively white, and everything else so gray.

I remembered only too well how I felt when I left Scotland and immigrated to Canada. I had such a deep ache inside. Loneliness. A sense of isolation. No old Glasgow friends. No family. Nothing was familiar. It was overwhelming even though I spoke the same language *and* I had the same color of skin as most of the locals. Oh, how I ached for home! Homesickness is real, and it is awful. I wondered if Janet suffered from it, or had she embraced the excitement of this chapter in her life? Did she dive into the Irish experience or sit alone in a small damp room in the hostel in Belfast?

The Queen Mary's Hostel is now called The Queen Mary's Hall. It is run by the Young Women's Christian Association. I stood outside wondering if this was where Frankie was conceived. Just to be standing here set off my sparking imagination. I imagined her coming home from her studies. I wonder what she was wearing. Did she dress like the fashion at that time or was she wearing wild African print dresses? I imagine her clicking her heels against the gray pavement while walking the two-minute walk from the University campus. How did she walk? Did she have that hip-swinging swagger that many African ladies have? I wondered if Frankie's dad walked her home in the late evenings after study. In my imagination he was handsome, tall, and intelligent. He wore a suit. For some reason, I never imagined him in African dress but I did imagine him filling Janet's head with romantic notions and basically seducing her.

It was only a bus ride to the vibrant city center, now full of trendy shops, cafés and restaurants. I wondered if it was as cosmopolitan in the '60s. I thought about them going into town together at the weekend. Was this African couple accepted in a predominantly white Belfast or was there a tension in the air when they walked into a bar.

It started to rain again and Rony and I snuck under the doorway of the terraced house. I imagined her carrying an umbrella. I wondered if they used them in Uganda or if they just let themselves get wet knowing, unlike here, that the sun would soon be out again.

The Edwardian gray terrace house was typical of the long leafy quarter. I managed to blag my way into the hostel and get a look at some of the rooms. As I walked through the door, I had this strange feeling that Janet was actually with me. The rooms were drab, musty, uninviting and cold. I'm sure the curtains hadn't been changed since 1966, or even washed for that matter. The whole place reeked of the past, but not one I had pictured; there was nothing romantic about it. I had wanted it to be magical. I wanted the place that conceived the great Titanic and my brother to glisten like that big ship. I wanted to imagine Janet in love with her medical student, Frankie's dad. But my illusions were sinking as fast as that ill-fated cruise ship.

Perhaps I was doing the establishment an injustice. Perhaps in 1966 it was modern for its day. I'm sure it would have been much fresher in the '60s. I'm sure it was safe, comfortable and affordable. But it was tired now, run down. All I sensed was Janet as a frightened, lonely girl with a secret in her belly. My brother's mother lying there curled up in one of those miserable beds beside a window with bars on it, trying to stay warm. All I could imagine was how she must have fretted about her secret, the questions that might have filled her head and given her nightmares. Actually, I was starting to become a nightmare for Rony with all my unanswerable questions. I was present, but I wasn't. I was living with ghosts from the past, weighed down carrying a suitcase full of trauma that wasn't even rightfully mine to carry. What was the best thing to do for her baby, for herself? Did she tell anyone? Did the father help her? Did anyone help? How on earth did this little Ugandan lady get herself from Belfast to Glasgow on her own when she was pregnant? She must have had to hide her belly while she was studying. I sat and worked out the months in my head. Frankie was born in late September. Schools would just be going back. She'd be at her biggest during the holidays. I hoped she didn't have to hide away in one of these dreadful rooms. The rooms were holding onto that secret. I wanted answers. The walls knew what Janet was thinking but they gave over nothing, nothing but the smell of the past.

Maybe my rightful place was to leave that past where it belonged. Take a step back. I had looked at the depths of Janet and Frankie's pain and I felt it. If I had honored their suffering, maybe I should respectfully bow down to it and bow out of this desire to dig deeper into someone else's past pain.

I had never been to Belfast, but I had always assumed it would be much like Glasgow. And I found they were somewhat similar, perhaps because they were both primarily shipbuilding cities. The biggest difference is the fierce sectarianism between the Catholics and the Protestants that fueled the Troubles. Of course, Glasgow has borne witness to sectarianism, too, but thankfully it has never suffered the intense violence that Northern Ireland did. Prejudice, distrust, and fear on both sides were rife in Belfast in the '60s. Did Janet suffer from any racial abuse? I had heard about the ghetto—streets and roads and whole areas of tremendous discrimination—but was the tension internal or would Janet have found herself in a city where sectarianism spilt over to the treatment of blacks?

In general, Frankie suffered very little racial discrimination in Glasgow, but there was always the odd occasion when someone would have a problem with the color of his skin. I remember a party Frankie and I were at with friends. It was one of the most terrifying nights of my life. The party was going full swing: underage teenagers drinking heavily, dancing, snogging and generally having a good time. Suddenly some bloke runs up to me yelling, "Quick! Someone's trying to stab Frankie!" He grabbed my hand and we both ran out onto the street to see this group of thugs semi circling Frankie and one bloke wielding a small knife. It was absolutely terrifying. I was hysterical, in tears and ran to his side. He was calm and told me to stay back. I was yelling and sobbing. "Please, leave him alone!" Some of our friends tried to intervene, even the friends of the guy with the knife were shouting, "Just leave the black bastard alone. He's not worth it!" Frankie was calm and said he didn't want any trouble. It all happened so fast. A large group of our friends quickly appeared and someone pulled me back from the group trying to protect me. I actually can't remember how it all seemed to calm down eventually. When the group of thugs left, I remember everyone let out the breath they had been holding and the party carried on. Frankie wanted to stay on and show a bit of bravado. All our friends were patting him on the back, "Well done, mate." "You showed that wanker where to go." I was scared the thugs could come back and I didn't leave his side. I was *so* glad when we got home that night. We never told our parents. I knew how much it would worry them. My parents were always really cool about us going out but I knew it worried them. I was always nervous at clubs, pubs and parties that some trouble would break out because of color.

Rony and I nipped into a traditional Irish pub for lunch. My fretting over the troubles of Belfast and racial tensions was quickly driven out by Irish hospitality. Everyone was having fun. It was Friday lunchtime. The chat and the drinks were flowing, laughter rattling off the antique tiled walls. The pub's music reminded me that at heart, the Irish are Celts, just like the Scots. I reassured myself that Janet would have made friends without any problems. I imagined this young African lady learning Irish jigs, swirling and twirling, laughing and drinking something stronger than African tea— probably for the first time in her life.

I began to think there would have been plenty of women in Ireland who swirled and twirled, laughed and drank and got themselves into trouble with men. I convinced myself that these women would have tried to help Janet with her little secret and would have understood her predicament, perhaps only too well. But then I frightened myself again by remembering those terrible convents that had been in the press recently, "the naughty girls' homes." Many described them as homes of horror. They were run by nuns. Most often parents sent their sinful daughters there for getting pregnant out of wedlock. Very few *ever* got out of the home—even as adults. The most infamous were the Magdalene asylums for 'fallen women' where young girls were forced to give up their illegitimate babies for adoption. Mother and child were separated, never to be seen or heard of again. Many had their babies simply taken from them and buried somewhere. The women and girls were ruled by prayers, chores, and all forms of cruel punishment and ritual humiliation. They were also forced to do hard labor in the laundry rooms of the convents and asylums where they washed clothes and linens for major hotel groups, the Irish Armed Forces and the brewer Guinness. Did Janet go to one of them? Was she sent there? Had she been told she *must* give up her child? Did she suffer their severe disapproval and condemnation of her sinful ways? Was she told a single mother was not fit to have a child and that she was a "fallen woman?" Did they turn her away because she was black? Is that why she chose to come to Scotland, to take that journey on the boat while pregnant? Was she alone?

I couldn't stop thinking about the moment in Thornhill Hospital in Paisley when Janet had to hand her baby over. I imagined her crying out, "Please don't take my baby!" The scene in my head was gut-wrenching. Surely every fiber of Janet's body was ready to receive Frankie as a baby—psychologically as well as physiologically. She must have been left with a dark void of despair and grief.

The grief for any mother to lose a child at birth must be horrendous. For a mother to give away her living, breathing child she just gave birth to must also be horrifying. The grief of knowing her baby is out there somewhere in the world without her—perhaps forever—must feel overwhelmingly desperate. The child is gone, yet not. There is no grave to visit, no memorial to honor the child, no friends and family to mourn your loss with. In this case, all Janet had was a shameful secret to carry with her all her days. Perhaps she, too, made up stories to soothe herself in her darkest moments: a story that perhaps her son had been lucky and was adopted by a wealthy, kind family in the UK and was thriving in a Western world. Maybe at other times, her stories were not so sweet. Perhaps she feared he had been left in some terrible children's home, the only black child which no one in Scotland wanted. I doubt she imagined he would ever turn up at her doorstep in Uganda for a warm reunion. Why was I so emotional about this woman who was not even my mother? Why couldn't I let it go?

Rony bought me another glass of wine and told me to try and enjoy the weekend, to stop worrying so much about something that happened in the past to a woman I didn't even know. He was right, of course, but I still couldn't stop thinking about her.

Then Rony said, "Look, I don't want to burst your bubble, babes, but maybe Janet didn't care that much. Maybe she was happy to get rid of an unwanted burden. Why do you have so much sympathy for her?" It sounded so cruel, but it was a good question. What if she was only thinking of herself and making her own life easier?

I felt prickly at Rony for bringing those callous thoughts to my attention. I knew full well that my dad was one of the rare adoptees whose biological mother had absolutely no regard for him, until he got himself a degree and she got herself drunk. Perhaps it was bizarre that I believed Frankie's mother was a good person, a compassionate mother doing the best for her child, when I knew only too well that can sometimes not be the case.

The YWCA was just down the road from Queen's University, our next destination. I assumed Janet and her lover would have graced its halls as students. Maybe they met at a student dance – perhaps at a cèilidh organized to introduce all the foreign students to one another. I imagined Janet and her charming medical student trying to follow the steps and becoming unwittingly entwined in each other's arms. They must have both been lonely, cold. One night they snuggled up together and one thing led to another. Oh, yes. The Victorian corridors of Queen's University were much more in keeping with my romantic notions of Frankie's conception!

At Queen's University, Rony and I spoke to a receptionist. The look on her face told me she'd just received the strangest inquiry of her career. However, she was sympathetic and made a series of phone calls trying to find us someone who could help. After some talks with some very obliging staff, I somehow managed to arrange a late afternoon meeting with a Dr. Eric Morier-Genoud in a coffee shop across the street from the university.

Eric was a lecturer in African and Imperial History and he was writing a paper on the African students who came to Belfast to study after many of the African colonies gained independence. He listened to my story with great interest and was generous with his time; he even told me he would try his best to trace Frankie's parents. I left Belfast that weekend grateful to have seen where Frankie was conceived and humbled that this professor had taken an interest in my story. There was none of the romantic sparkle I had pictured and hoped for, but there was now a spark of hope that Eric would be able to find for me some information about Frankie's parents.

CHAPTER TWO
Twins

Scotland, 1967

Born a month apart in 1966, Frankie and I were raised as twins. Our parents pushed us down Byres Road in the West End of Glasgow in a twin pram: one black child and one white child inside. Dad had always had a strong desire to adopt. He wanted to a give a vulnerable child a home and the love that was missing from his own child-hood. Mum, on the other hand had some serious reser-vations about adoption. In fact, Dad had to talk her into it. However, I think two little Pakistani children probably helped my dad's case. Mum once told me that before I was born, they almost adopted two Pakistani siblings. Their mother had been brought over from Pakistan for an arranged marriage to the local grocery shopkeep-er. He already had a white girlfriend but had to marry someone from his own faith. They married in Glasgow and had two children. However, very sadly, this young mother's sari caught fire on the small barred heater in her flat. She was unable to remove herself from the sari and burned to death. My parents were told that the two small children watched in horror as their mum died in front of them. Mum and Dad had gotten to know the family fairly well as the shop was close by and were devastated when they heard what had happened. The grocery shopkeeper had to work all hours day and night and so my parents offered to look after the two young siblings. Their father rarely came by to check on them. He seemed to have more interest in his white mistress. As the months went by, my mum and dad grew very fond of these children and considered adopting them. However, in the end the grandfather came over from Pakistan and took the children back home with him. Amongst my inherited paperwork I found a letter from the grandfather thanking my parents for all they had done for his grandchildren. My parents had kept it all those years and I still have it. Mum told me she often wondered what happened to them. I think perhaps the love she found in her heart for these two beautiful children made her feel she could adopt.

I'm not sure exactly when my parents started the adoption process but I know they hadn't set out to adopt a black child. What they had wanted to do was to adopt a "hard to place" child, one who was perhaps older than a newborn, had a disability, or had been removed from an abusive situation. My older brother Stephen was eight at the time. Initially, my parents had thought a child of perhaps three or four might be a good idea so the adopted child would be in-between our ages. It was attractive to the adoption agency because that age group was rarely considered; most couples looking to adopt at that time wanted a newborn. However, when a little black boy arrived at Tanker Ha' Children's Home in Kilmarnock, Scotland, he proved to be *very* hard to place. This little boy was now thirteen months old and seemed destined to be left behind.

My parents were asked if they would consider a black child. Now, this was 1967—the height of the American Civil Rights Movement. Martin Luther King was never out of the news. In some parts of Britain, racial tension had reached the boiling point with some landlords refusing to rent to the "nig-nogs" and some hairdressers even refusing to cut their hair.

The strange thing is, I don't believe either of my parents had any hesitation about the color of a child's skin. I think, with Frankie, it truly was love at first sight. Mum later confessed, laughing with me, that her biggest concern was how to comb his hair.

Our beautiful mum

However, the adoption agency had bigger concerns. With only weeks between Frankie and I in age, they felt there could be territorial issues. So, Frankie came into our home as a foster child. Thankfully there were no territorial issues at all. From what Mum and Dad said, Frankie followed me around everywhere and I guided him like a toddler-mother. Any fears were quashed and he was legally adopted into our family less than a year later.

Pushing a black and a white child in a twin pram in Glasgow in the '60s was unusual, to say the least. According to Mum, we caused a bit of a stir wherever we went. Everyone wanted to stop Mum in the street and *goo goo gah gah* over her new little black baby. They wanted to touch his coarse, curly hair and feel his skin. Sadly for Mum, some of this touching and prodding and adoration of her new black son was too much. One day, when she was near death, she confessed to me that she had wanted to scream at these well-meaning people surrounding her, "What about *my* new baby? What about Michaela? Haven't *I* produced my own gorgeous, cute, little baby girl?"

It seemed to her that everyone was only interested in the poor little black boy and not at all in her own daughter. Frankie would get handed free sweeties in the sweetie shop and bits of sweet dumpling in the local butcher's, and they seemed to forget about me. I'm not telling you this because I am looking for sympathy. I don't remember too much about it, but Mum obviously did, and it was still painful for her to admit. I think she felt guilty for feeling upset about it. When she told me, I cried with her, but the tears were for her pain. I told her I wasn't bothered and I really wasn't; it wasn't until later that night, after I downed a bottle of wine on my own, that it hit me.

I always felt I had to try hard to make people like me and that there was some basic flaw in me. Frankie could walk into a room and people would flock to him. People would talk about how his smile lit up a room and what a wonderful laugh he had. Both were true! Frankie didn't have to do anything for most people to like him. It was apparent with friends, with teachers, and also with some relatives. Mum admitted to me, "I used to get so angry, did people think we starved him and put him in a dark cellar or something? They were always feeling sorry for him and offering him things as if he didn't get anything at home. Everyone always wanted to touch him and cuddle him like he was a soft toy. You would be sitting right beside him and people would just go directly to him. Why couldn't they look at you? Want to pick you up? I sometimes felt they treated him like he was a pet and not a child."

Add to this the fact that everyone felt Frankie was special; he had been chosen by my parents and was a gift from God to our family. This sugary sentiment is understandable. After all, this little child needed all the love and attention my parents, and everyone around, could give him. He'd been abandoned. Everyone felt awful about that and somehow wanted to make it better for him. He was black in a sea of white strangers. And the wee soul couldn't even hide the fact that he was adopted because in the '60s that's what people did. Adoption was cloaked in secrecy.

I never saw any of this till Mum started to talk about her feelings that day. It wasn't something she usually did. She generally kept most of her pain to herself, but when she was dying, we talked a lot, and it was obvious that when it came to Frankie, she wanted to get some things off her chest.

I did cry that night. I cried hard—a primal wail. One of those on-the-floor-kinds of wails. It wasn't for Mum...or Frankie. It was for me.

I couldn't remember those earlier years in the pram, just like Frankie did not remember the day he was separated from his mum. Psychologists talk about the first three years of life being the most important for emotional development, and the fact that a child has no tangible memory, does not lessen the impact of those early experiences. Indeed, they can have a profound devastating effect on the future of the child.

The severing of the connection to one's mother from birth *must* trigger a grieving process for both mother and child. The sheer despair that must be felt by both is almost unfathomable. At some level, the memory of that severance must haunt the child as much as it must the mother. The unconscious fears of further losses and rejections have to somehow manifest themselves. I can only imagine the terror an infant must feel at being unceremoniously taken from the mother whose very womb they depended on for life just minutes before.

While Frankie had a smile that could charm all of Scotland, I was always aware of his pain below the surface. I was haunted by Frankie's terrifying screams as an infant. You see, just as we were getting ready to leave the house in the pram Frankie would scream blue murder. His anxiety was immense and there was no pacifying him. Mum told me that when she opened the door she had to close it again for fear of the neighbors thinking she was murdering him. She told me it took ages to get us out the door, and when we did finally make it over the threshold, Frankie was always in a state of panic.

Although I can't remember this in detail, I know in a strange way I have absorbed it; I have an image of us side by side in the pram, me sensing his anxiety and wanting to help him. Calm him. Tell him not to be scared. But I was only thirteen months old too. God, I am upset writing this. It must be a memory. Imagine me, a baby, hearing those terrifying, anxious screams. If they scared Mum, they must have scared me too.

It's sad to think Frankie probably thought he was going to be abandoned again. When Frankie first came to stay with us, it was only for a few nights here and there to see how he would adjust to his new home and how I would adjust to having him there. Looking back, I am not sure those well-meaning social workers got it right. Anytime he left our house he probably thought he was going to be sent back to the children's home. It was evident he did not want to go back there; his screams were his way of fighting for his survival. And Mum was his key to survival.

Mum said she didn't realize how difficult it would be to have an adopted child, especially a black one. I don't think the social workers ever considered the fact that the mother might be the one resentful of the attention a black child could take from her own child. Add to this the complexity of adoption itself and I think it set off a chain of emotional responses and ambivalent behavior.

Perhaps she, like many, naively thought adopting a child wouldn't be unlike having her own biological child. But how could it when the very child you are bringing into your home is in a state of grief for their biological mother? The substitute mother most certainly has her work cut out for her. And if she doesn't understand some of the emotional complexities going on, she can, as I think Mum often did, find herself an innocent victim of them.

Even from a toddler, it seemed Frankie was unconsciously programmed to push all her buttons. Yet *she* was the very person he wanted more than anyone else in the world to love him. She was his lifeline. He adored her. But, as time went on, his need of her seemed to drive him to do the very things that would upset her the most. I think she was 'tested' over and over again by Frankie to see if she would reject him. Deep down I believe he perceived his own mother rejected him because he was a *bad* baby and defective in some way. If only Frankie could have believed he was special and that my mum loved him, things might have been different. However, the deep fear of unworthiness that few saw made even a hint of rejection catastrophic, yet he couldn't help but perpetuate his own fears. I think this behavior gave rise to Mum feeling guilty for not being good enough as his mother. She once said to me, "Why would he do things to upset me if I was a good enough mum?" Deep down Mum felt she had failed as his mother. Of course, she hadn't. It was his very love of her that caused his anxiety and tension. He was making it almost impossible for her to love him as she would have wanted. I think the battle was exhausting for them both at times.

I am so glad Mum opened up to me when she did and told me how she had felt, even if she thought it made her sound cold. It brought to light some of the issues she was dealing with. Sadly, there was little to no help back then for Mum, even if she had confessed her feelings at the time. She was not fully equipped to deal with some of the consequences of adopting a child, let alone a black child in the '60s, but she most certainly did her best.

Maybe all this was what had drawn me to the stage. Even as I child I was always putting on dance displays and singing for my parents and their friends. I suppose it was my way of getting attention. But I never had the confidence to take it to the next level—until Frankie died.

Fairy Tales and the Death of Innocence

Whenever I was sad or needed to work things through, I wrote. At the time Frankie died, my writing became songs, and so I penned a song for Frankie and put music to it. I tried to do a home recording to send back to the family in Scotland, but it just didn't sound good enough. I wanted it to be special. Eventually, I plucked up the courage to book time at a local recording studio in Ottawa called Raven Street Studios. I had never recorded before and had no idea how long it would take. The studio had package deals, so I decided to go for the three-hour package. When I got there, I was *incredibly* nervous. I was introduced to the sound engineer Steve Tevlin. Steve was a tall, laid back bloke and did his best to put me at ease. However, seeing the concert grand piano and all the studio equipment and various recording booths was intimidating. Steve sat me down at the piano and allowed me time to get familiar with the keys while he set up the microphone and adjusted the sound levels. A short while later he was ready to start recording. I sang the song and played the piano at the same time. After I was finished, much to my surprise, Steve said through the headphones, "That sounded great. Want to come through and hear it?"

Performing at the Cannes Film Festival

Steve played it back. I was so surprised! My voice sounded much deeper than I thought and sounded enormous over the big studio speakers. It was quite something to hear it being played back to me for the first time in a studio. I kept saying, "Is that me; is that really what I sound like?" Steve assured me he hadn't used any tricks and it was indeed me. He asked if I had any other songs as I had booked three hours. So, unrehearsed I sat back down at the piano and recorded six songs I had written.

A few days later I got a call from Breen Murray, the owner of the studio, asking me to meet him to discuss a contract. I talked to a few musicians and their advice was to send the recording to some record companies before signing with a studio. I did and much to my astonishment, Bonnie Fedrau, an Artists and Repertoire talent scout from Warren Records at the time, called me and said she loved it! But she wanted to hear what kind of sound I was looking for and asked me to do a full demo track with a band and send it to her. So, I worked on a demo with a fabulous local musician and producer, James Stephens, and then started sending it out. Within a relatively short time frame, much to my amazement, I had won some songwriting competitions, including the Majic100 Radio station Songwriter's competition. I therefore got a fair bit of radio play. Bonnie had by then moved to EMI records and managed to bring the EMI president out to hear me play a solo gig in Toronto. That night the champagne got opened. He loved my performance!

Within a year of Frankie's death, I was dealing with producers and record companies in Toronto. The following year, I left my day job in a clothing store in Ottawa, signed a production deal with Juno award-winning producer Greg Kavanagh and headed to Toronto to produce my first album.

There were days after Frankie's death I thought I would never live again. It felt like I was in a posture of mourning and always would be. During that time, having my music to focus on was such a blessing. It took my greatest loss in life to fulfill a dream and create a new beginning. It was like a fairy tale.

But, like all fairy tales, they have tremendous highs and tremendous lows. During the recording of the album, my dad died of Hepatitis C which he had contracted through bad blood given to him during open heart surgery twelve years previously. When I was ten years old, my dad had a massive heart attack in front of me and I had always lived in fear of his death. You can never prepare yourself. I was distraught at losing my dad so soon after Frankie. One of my greatest disappointments in life is that my dad died having never seen me perform on stage or heard my CD. Dad loved to write, like me, he was always scribbling away and often sent me some lyrics to put music to. Two of those songs we did together I wanted to include in the album.

I was working in the studio and knew Dad wasn't well. Greg and I were rushing to get those two tracks finished so I could mail them to Dad. That afternoon Greg got a call from EMI; someone much more important than me needed a remix of a song done right away. Greg told me I might as well go back to Ottawa, as he'd be working on it all week. However, he made sure he produced a mix of the two songs for my dad and handed them to me as I was leaving. I put them in my coat pocket, and just as I was about to leave he said, "If you're about to mail those to your dad, don't. Just take them home first and make sure they are okay. I'm having problems with my recording machine."

When I arrived back in Ottawa that night, I got a distressing call from Mum saying she didn't think my dad had long. My husband and I booked a flight and left the next day. When I arrived home, Dad was clearly near death. It was devastating to see him like that. I took the recording from my pocket and played the two songs for him. He was unable to speak but tears ran down his cheeks and I knew he had heard them. He died the following morning.

Despite the overwhelming loss of my dad, I recognized that if EMI had not called requesting Greg to work on an urgent job, I wouldn't have been home in Ottawa with my husband when I got that dreaded call from my mum. And, if Greg had not told me at the last minute *not* to mail the recordings, my dad would have never heard them. It was, in fact, miraculous.

After Dad died, I knew Mum didn't want me to leave Scotland, and I certainly didn't want to go, but she wanted me to finish the CD and pursue my dreams. At times, I felt I was perhaps living the kind of life she secretly yearned for, a life of creative expression. She would often say, "I wish I had your guts in life." Yet, most often, I was trembling inside.

Working on the CD gave me focus. Though I was still grieving for my dad, Greg brightened my days in the studio. He was not only a wonderful producer, but a really nice guy with a great sense of humor. But, in the end, I think the raw, emotional energy of my grief is evident in that CD, *Fairy Tales and The Death of Innocence*.

However, once the CD was complete, the record deal that EMI had as much as *promised* was pulled from the table. They didn't feel the album was commercial enough. At the time, I was crestfallen. There was so much buzz around me and the CD in the industry. It was also embarrassing, and I felt like a failure. But I knew the business could be that harsh. Thankfully, I still had my fan base, and so we decided to release the CD independently with a major independent distribution deal. Shortly after, we won a grant to produce a music video—which at that time was not something everyone could do as it was very expensive.

The album did reasonably well; we got some airplay and thanks to the publicist, Jane Harbury, we got a fair amount of media attention. I started to fill venues and open for some bigger players. I traveled, sang, played and basically lived and breathed my songwriting through those years. I always felt blessed to work with tremendously talented musicians and performed various gigs with members of the Ottawa Symphony Orchestra. For someone who only studied to grade two in music and failed that exam, it was pretty incredible. I even managed to get a few tracks on film and TV.

I never gave up and went on to produce two more CDs. With my third album, I got to work with both Russian genius composer Kirill Shirokov and Rolf Soja of *Yes Sir, I Can Boogie* fame. I couldn't believe I was working with Rolf and writing lyrics to his music. As a child, I must have played that record and danced in my living room a million times! Rolf and his co-writers had basically saved RCA's ass with that song in the '70s. RCA was eventually acquired by BMG and the song was still making them money in 2006! Rolf was a fan of my music, but he didn't think it was commercial enough to push the glass ceiling. He also felt Kirill was a brilliant composer and we worked well together. So Kirill, Rolf and I worked on producing a commercial album for BMG. Rolf was convinced it would fly and had the powers to be in place.

Exactly the same thing happened with my most "commercial" CD as happened with EMI. Rolf couldn't believe that after sending them song after song and being told the album sounded great and they wanted it, in the end they wouldn't sign me. They thought I was too old and instead signed a seventeen-year-old. It was a total kick in the teeth, not only for me, but for Rolf and Kirill.

Did I make a lot of money? No, but I was rich with experience—meeting people from all walks of life, traveling, and doing what I loved. I even left the safety net of the Toronto music scene at one point to live in New York City for six months. I wheeled my keyboard through the streets of the East Village, often at 3:00 a.m. and sometimes having only played to a room of five people. That's not an unusual story for any struggling artist, but it felt pretty amazing that I had the guts to go there and try to do it on my own. It was an incredible experience *and* a lesson in humility.

However, ironically after Mum died and I had my breakthrough moment with the bottle of wine, I only gave a few more concerts. Maybe I needed time out to mourn and work through what my new life was going to look like now that I had lost all my key family. I am not saying this to pull out reader sympathy. I don't need it or want it. I am writing this book for a reason.

After Mum died, I used to sleep in her bed. It made me feel close to her. One night I decided to watch a movie. I opened the video player and the 1983 Grace Kelly movie with Cheryl Ladd was still in the machine. It must have been the last film she watched from her bed. My mum adored Grace Kelly and had watched every film she ever made. She loved the fairy tale story of the beautiful actress who married Prince Rainier of Monaco. She had always wanted to go to Monaco but sadly never did. I watched the movie that night and had a good cry.

A few months later, out of the blue, I got a call from the organizers of the Monaco Film Festival. To my absolute surprise, they wanted me to sing at the festival! The festival was for non-violent films and I was to sing at the Angel Awards. I was told I would be performing at the Hotel Hermitage. I was so excited I could hardly believe it. Then a month or so before the event I got another call. This time Rosana, the director of the festival, asked if I would like to be the ambassador for the Film Festival. It sounded so prestigious—I wasn't sure I was the person for the job. Didn't you have to be clever to be an ambassador? At school, I was told I was a slow learner. A diagnosis of dyslexia didn't come till much later in my life. Rosana told me they had been playing my music a lot and felt my lyrics were pertinent to the event. She was sure I'd be perfect. She reassured me that I would only have to give a few short speeches. I still wasn't sure I was *ambassador* material but just as I was about to hang up, Rosana said, "Oh, Michaela, by the way, we've changed the venue for your performance. It is going to be at the Princess Grace Theatre. I hope that's okay. I think you'll like it." Like it. I was stunned! All I could think about was Mum. I knew then she was with me and would be every single step of the way in Monaco. It was like her gift to me, to her, for all we had been through less than a year before. It was like another fairy tale come true.

Subsequently, I was invited to sing at the Cannes Film Festival, which was also an incredible experience. However, it was perhaps a turning point.

The reviews were great. Nothing negative happened but gradually, the need to perform seemed to leave me. There are many possible explanations for that. Perhaps I was only ever performing for my mum's attention and to make her happy. Or perhaps I recognized, after those conversations with Mum about Frankie, that I didn't have to practice the piano for eight hours a day, do vocal warm-ups every morning, twist my guts in two and sometimes throw up before going on stage—all just to get people to like me. The immediate gratification of praise from performing seemed no longer necessary. But writing was.

My songs were always driven by the lyrics. The fact that I could layer music on top was the icing on the cake and I *loved* it. But I wanted to dig deeper, to be alone and stretch my writing skills. It didn't matter if it reached an audience at that point. It felt like my soul was crying out for more space on the page and not the stage. But for someone who had been told they were stupid by a teacher, I needed more guts to attempt a novel than it took to sing at Monaco and Cannes.

Within a year of Mum's passing, everything changed. I left my husband, I left Canada, and I moved back to Scotland. All my old safety nets were gone: my family, my husband, my career. Like all transitions, it was horrendous but necessary. It was a painful metamorphosis. For a while, I tried to hold onto a past that was no longer available to me. It was terrifying to finally let go. For me, death has always brought about a kind of death of self and a rebirth of some kind. Endings are the other side of beginnings. I couldn't see the future as yet but I had to put my faith in the mystery of it all.

CHAPTER THREE

Breakfast—Children on the Menu

Uganda, 2012

Where we are staying is a magnet for bishops, pastors, the clergy and the born-again. You can't have breakfast without getting a sermon along with your cereal.

Rony turns around to the purple-robed Bishop flailing his arms and asking *What Would Jesus Do* and says, "He'd tell you to be quiet—I'm having my cornflakes."

The Bishop draws him a look of disdain and carries on delivering his thoughts to the diners on the outside balcony.

A well-dressed African man takes a seat at our table. He snaps his fingers and summons a waiter to take his order. He reaches across the table and shakes Rony's hand, then mine. I can't help but see the Rolex watch he's flashing. I wonder if it's as fake as his grin and his perfect row of white veneers.

"I'm Gilbert. I couldn't help noticing you both. I was just wondering what brings you to Uganda."

I've been watching this vulture scan the tables in this room for the past few days and have seen how he slides up to his innocent prey: usually, a wide-eyed gull-

59

ible Christian couple looking to adopt a baby—the place is full of them. But now he has descended on our table.

I tell him I'm here because I am writing a novel. I hope that will send him flapping off in another direction.

"Oh really...a novel...how very interesting." He shuffles his seat in closer. "I saw you both visiting the Babies' Home the other day and thought perhaps you were considering adopting."

"No. But my brother was adopted. He was Ugandan. We're just helping out at the Babies' Home."

He fans out his napkin. "Oh. Really. That is very interesting. Very interesting indeed. How much did your brother cost?"

I almost choke on my breakfast. "Excuse me! We didn't *buy* him. He was abandoned in Scotland and my parents adopted him there. They didn't pay *anything* for my brother."

My face isn't just red from the sun. Rony puts his hand on my leg and gives it a light squeeze. He knows I'm angry at this guy's suggestion that my parents bought Frankie.

"Oh. I'm sorry. It's just that there are so many – muzungus—I mean white people—who come here to adopt children. It can be very costly these days and a long process, unless you know the right people. I'm a lawyer." He leans in closer. "I can help *expedite* things, if you know what I mean."

Sadly, I do know what he means. I've heard about the shady deals getting done with adoptions in this country. *The Madonna Syndrome* has been as big a hit as her records, with little black babies *selling* as well as they do. I'm beginning to realize there are as many holes in the legal system as in the worn-out mosquito net hung above my guest room bed.

"I'm sorry to disappoint you, Gilbert, but I'm afraid we're *not* here to adopt."

He grins and reaches into his breast pocket. "Well, if you ever change your mind, here's my card. Just give me a call. Adoption is my specialty."

He says it like a chef who only has children on his menu. I leave his card sitting in the middle of the table.

His English-style breakfast arrives and he picks up his knife and fork. "I do criminal law too. I'm working on a big case right now. A very big case. Child sacrifice—have you heard about that?"

We nod in unison.

Rony and I have just come back from Luweero where we were told some villagers still believe in child sacrifice. It was explained to us that most of the children are scarred or pierced somewhere to protect them from the witch doctors, as they will only sacrifice a perfect child. It seems wealthy businessmen pay thousands of dollars to the witch doctors to hunt down impoverished children to harvest their body parts, which many believe can cure impotence and increase wealth.

As Gilbert slices up his breakfast, he tells us he is prosecuting a wealthy businessman who had a witch doctor cut a child in four pieces. Each section of the child's body was placed under a corner of the man's new hotel building in the belief that it would create more riches for him. Gilbert puts his cutlery down and says, "But you know what this man did? Eh, Eh?" He wipes his chin with his napkin. "I will tell you what he did. He bought off the judge and jury and the case was thrown out. Just like that!" He snaps his fingers for effect.

He picks up his cutlery again and points his fork at me. "But I am a determined guy. I went to the top." He points his fork in the air. "I went to M7."

We look at him quizzically.

61

"Museveni. You know, our President. We call him M7. Well, I got an appeal from him. We are back in court soon. Let us hope and pray this guy does not pay off the parents. That is what these rich guys usually do." He cuts into another piece of sausage and carries on describing the brutal nature of some of the sacrifices: how these witch doctors snatch innocent children on their way home from school or while fetching water and how they sever their limbs and genitals.

I can't bear any more. I turn to Rony, "Is it too early for a brandy?"

Later that day, we are back at the Babies' Home, helping out, when I overhear an American woman shouting.

I look over to see the family who I know is in the process of adopting a two-year-old black child from the Home. The mother is shouting at her white daughter, who looks to be about ten years old.

I have noticed this girl before as she never wants to play, preferring to look huffy and sit on her own. Now she's being told by her mother that she *has* to play with her new brother. "He's going to be part of our family whether you like it or not, young lady. Now go and get your brother. Pick him up and bring him over here."

The previous day, I had asked this same woman what made her want to come to Uganda to adopt a child? She answered in her Southern drawl, "Oh my friend along our street had adopted one and I thought it was a cool thing to do. She was so cute, you know, and well, I really think the Lord wants me to do this, to give a child a good home. I already have a girl, so I thought a boy would be a nice addition." She cuddles her new son to be. "What do you think? Isn't Henry *goooorgeous*?" She's talking about this child like she has just picked out a new handbag. She bounces him on her knee. "It won't be long now Henry. Soon you'll be in your new home. With your new mommy and daddy."

I wonder if this woman would care if she were to be told that perhaps Henry has parents who may want him back.

In the short time I have been here I am beginning to see a really dark side to adoption. It's difficult to know for sure how many children are actually full orphans.

The term orphan in Africa used to mean a child without both parents. However, today, in most of Africa it doesn't necessarily mean the child is without parents. Often the child has been put into care because the family cannot afford to keep the child at that moment in time, but they plan to come back for the child as soon as they can see their way clear to support their child. Perhaps the mother has died, and the father has to work full time to support his other children and cannot take care of a baby. Or perhaps the father has left the marital home or married another woman and the mother cannot cope financially.

Ugandans have big families. There must be more desirable ways of providing support to the existing family and getting the child reunited with his or her family. Surely putting them in a Babies' Home should be the last resort.

I ask this adoptive mother if she would mind telling me how much the adoption cost. I pretend I am potentially interested in adopting myself.

"Oh... I think...all in...about twenty thousand dollars."

"That's a lot of money." I remark.

"Yes, it sure is. But our church back home helped us raise it all, you know." She holds Henry up in the air. "I can't wait to take him back and show him to the congregation!"

I could just imagine the scene back home at church, parading little Henry as the saved child brought from poverty into the care of this wonderful new Christian family in America.

I ask, "Is it a difficult process to go through?"

"Not really. We have a great lawyer helping us and the matron's been *so* great. We only met little Henry three weeks ago." She laughs. "We're supposed to live here, in Uganda, for three *years* before we can adopt, but our lawyer knows a loop hole; he's *so* good that way. We've been granted guardianship by the High Court of Uganda. As long as we intend to adopt Henry once he is with us in the States, we can leave Uganda with him in a few days."

"Wow. Are you sure about that?" I ask.

"Oh, yeah. Our lawyer is a Christian. I trust him. If you're interested, I can give you his name. It's a miracle we found him."

I smile and take my leave.

I wouldn't want to insult the good intentions of some adoptive parents but I can't help but wonder if their philanthropic response would be so great without their social media feeds. I'm starting to add up how many people would be out of a job if these adoptions weren't taking place and these homes didn't exist. Some of the homes even charge room and board to the parents-to-be and the well-meaning tourists who help out at the homes. At an average of $80 a night, over a three-week period, that's a lot of cash.

But I'm thinking surely there are many Ugandans who wish to adopt. Ugandans all want big families. There *must* be families who can't conceive who would love to adopt but are getting bypassed in favor of the muzungus. Wealth alone, even relative wealth, cannot guarantee a better life for a child.

Muzungu is a Bantu word dating back to the 18th century, used in the African Great Lakes region to refer to people from Europe. It means "someone who roams around aimlessly." It seems 18th century explorers had a tendency to get lost when wandering in Africa. Nowadays it is used to refer to anyone with white skin. It is not necessarily a derogatory term; traditionally, people with white skin in Africa were considered wealthy and that belief continues today.

I'm beginning to sense that well-meaning muzungus are unwittingly feeding into an orphan tourism industry. It seems inter-country adoption has become vastly lucrative, with children as commodities. I'm sure most of these people are driven by compassion and a desire to help, especially after witnessing the levels of poverty. That's why I think we are all such easy targets and why I reckon *some* of these homes keep the babies and children looking so impoverished.

But it's not just the well-meaning people in search of a vulnerable child to adopt into their family that concerns me. If it's that easy to "buy" children and bring them out of the country, surely they are at risk of sex tourism or child pornography.

The solemn young daughter drags herself over to her new brother and reluctantly picks him up. It's an uncomfortable scene to witness. I can sense the girl's scorn at having to accommodate her new brother, or is it her mother's whims she is accommodating? I want to speak to the girl and ask her how *she* feels about this adoption and her new brother to be. There is so much fuss being made around the new adopted sibling. I wonder if her feelings have even been considered in this adoption.

It makes me wonder about my older brother Stephen. I know Stephen was not rejected by our parents in favor of Frankie or me, but I also know he certainly didn't appreciate the day I appeared in the world. I wonder if he felt shunned in some way by having *two* siblings the same age running around beneath his feet. Perhaps he felt we were a bit of a circus show—the black and white twins. I was always finding new ways to seek attention while Frankie was always unwittingly the center of it. Frankie, however, was never a victim of Stephen's disdain. I, on the other hand, was. Stephen, I am sure, has his own story. That is best left for him to share. Perhaps my greatest disappointment in life is that my biological brother and I have no relationship; we have never been close.

And perhaps too, Frankie subconsciously knew he had to make an ally of Stephen, and in his usual charming way, he did so. He was compliant with Stephen—something I was far from able to mimic. Frankie rarely showed anger, hostility, disappointment, or sadness and he could innocently garner pity. It is easy to get along with a sibling like that. I was the complete opposite. I readily showed my emotions. But then I didn't have the internal anxieties that Frankie had.

Frankie and me in the bathtub

Leaving the Past Where It Belongs

Scotland, 2011

My inbox pinged early in the morning—an email from Dr. Eric Morier-Genoud, whom I'd been hoping to hear from since my January weekend in Belfast. I looked out the window at the beautiful April morning—the sun shining, birds chirping, leaves starting to show on the trees. Maybe this was a sign of good things to come.

I wondered if I should wait until Rony woke up before reading the email. I felt this could be momentous: I so hoped Eric had been able to find Janet! Perhaps he had found both of Frankie's parents! I paced the floor, unable to wait any longer; I had to know. I said a prayer, then closed my eyes, hit the key, then slowly opened them enough to peek at the screen.

> *Dear Michaela,*
>
> *I am afraid to say that the University Student records could not find any trace of Janet. Here is what they said:*
>
> *"Unfortunately, we were unable to trace any records of Janet Weivugira (Wevugira).*
>
> *I have contacted another college (St. Mary) and they had no record of an African studying there. I am afraid I have stopped there. I contacted a certain Wevugira on Facebook but he was unrelated."*

I hope you have better luck in Uganda, as well as a safe and pleasant trip. Please do let me know if you find any traces of her.

Our report is advancing well and we are hopeful to be finished by the end of April. I will let you know about it.

Best wishes and again, a safe trip to Africa.
Eric.

Just like that, my spark of hope for finding Frankie's parents was extinguished. But how could it be? I could understand Janet producing an alias name for the father, but was she herself not on record as having been in Belfast? If Eric, who does extensive research on Africans in Belfast during the very time in question can't find a trace of them, what chance do I have? I was deflated. It was just as well Rony was still in bed. Perhaps I could recover before he got up.

Why did this seem so important in the first place? Janet gave up her child over forty-five years ago, so why was I digging around looking for her? What right had I to have even opened that folder? She wasn't *my* mother and even if I were to find her, Frankie would still be dead.

I needed to shake off my mood. A shower would help. I stared at the picture of Frankie and me in the bathtub as youngsters. It used to sit on top of our upright piano at home; now it had pride of place in my bathroom. I missed him *so* much. I missed all my family. I wondered if I was searching for his family now that I was technically an orphan myself. What piece of my life was truly so missing that I wanted to find this woman who gave birth to my brother? Was it that Frankie was so like a biological twin to me that I felt I had to carry on the search he had wanted to make in his last year of life?

The warm water from the shower merged with my tears.

My father always used to say, "Leave the past where it belongs." I kept hearing that phrase resounding in my head. I knew that is what I had to do, to leave the past where it belonged. I had to resign myself to the void of never knowing who Frankie's mother or father was.

I put my dressing gown back on, poured myself a coffee, went back to my desk and continued writing my novel. However, my life was soon to become stranger than fiction.

Hallowed Gates

Gayaza High School
Gayaza, Wakiso district,
Buganda Region, Uganda, 2012

The intimidating young guard doesn't speak but brandishes his rifle at Rony and me.

I take a step back from the gates. "I'm here to see Head Teacher Vicky Kisarale."

He smiles and relaxes his gun. "Ah, welcome to Gayaza High School. Any friend of Vicky's is a friend of mine."

The massive gates slowly creak open. We enter the grounds; it's like entering a bygone era. The gates close with a thud. I have the sudden feeling of being trapped in Gayaza, like it's a prison.

I'm swept back to the time I was singing at The Kingston Penitentiary for Women in Canada. I remember the large iron gates shutting behind me and being led by a woman with a rifle out to a beautiful lawn where I was to perform for women who were murderers. This is a school; still I feel a bit like I did that day—scared, but with a mix of excitement and curiosity.

I wonder if the young female students feel like this when they arrive here, knowing that they are expected to live and study in this one place throughout their high school years. It is such an honor for these girls to attend Gayaza, to even consider leaving would not be tolerated in Ugandan culture.

Gayaza High School is the oldest girl's school in Uganda. It is an iconic institution. It was set up in 1905 by a formidable group of female missionaries to educate the daughters of chiefs to become suitable wives. Now, just about all Ugandan families wish their daughters to be educated here. I'm disappointed that, as today is a school holiday, none of the students will be here to talk to or to see in their lovely red and white uniforms. But Vicky thought it best as it would give us more time to talk and for her to show me around.

We stroll up the long tree-lined path to Vicky's office. As a young teenager, I certainly wouldn't have coped with this kind of educational institution. I wasn't considered "clever" at school and wouldn't have been a candidate for such a lofty education. I was also far too attached to my home at that age—I would have hated being sent away to study as well as being separated from Frankie. I imagine myself being knocked down by the "clever" girls and wanting to call home every day. No, I was not Gayaza material.

I can sense history here—a history that I wonder if Frankie's family perhaps also belonged to.

At the end of the path sits a church. I want to go in and feel the atmosphere. I want to tour the bright green manicured lawns that sprawl before me, walk through the unfamiliar trees and the long colonial-style buildings. Much to my surprise and delight, many of the trees have a sign nailed on them which not only gives the name of the species but explains the purposes they can be used for. I *love* trees and start reading the properties of the various species. I learn that the olive-green, bushy, fern-like tree beside me is called Grevillea Robusta and is used for external joinery. It's also good for cabinet timber and is resistant to rotting. Then I spy a Mango Tree *pregnant* with its fleshy, rose- and lime-colored fruit. I read that its leaves and its bark cure coughs. I'm thinking maybe Rony should try some, but he has taken shade under a giant tree which seem to be ubiquitous here. It turns out he's standing under the Mvule tree which not only provides excellent shade but is one of Uganda's most valuable resources of good timber. I am busy taking in the sights and fragrances of the trees standing proud on the 140 acres surrounding us when we are greeted by the lovely Ugandan head teacher, Vicky. Her clothes are classic British—knee length skirt, checked shirt. She's generous with her smiles and puts me at ease right away, something very few head teachers have done in my life.

"Come, come." She ushers Rony and me into her 1950s-style office. "Tea?"

There is still something very British about the Ugandans and serving tea is part of that. I spy a picture of Sheelagh Warren on the mantel. Sheelagh Warren was the head teacher of Gayaza from the fifties to the eighties. And she is the other serendipitous reason I have found my way to these hallowed gates.

Serendipity

Canada, 2009

I was attending the induction of my friend Brian Galligan into the Anglican Priesthood in Canada and a group of us were staying at Brian's house in Milton, Ontario. His cousin Sheila is a librarian and she was curious about my writing. I told her the novel was set in Uganda and that it started around the time of Idi Amin.

Sheila was astonished and told me her friend had written a book about the Archbishop of Uganda, Janani Luwum. I couldn't believe it—I had just finished writing about Janani's murder in my novel. Janani was one of the most influential church leaders in the history of Uganda. Sheila went on to tell me her friend, Margaret Ford, was a nun and had been Janani's secretary at the time of his brutal murder. Later, it was discovered that Idi Amin had him stripped naked, beaten and then Amin shot him. Margaret had to make a harrowing escape from Uganda during the last and harshest days of Amin's reign.

I was surprised Sheila had a direct link to someone who was in Uganda at the very time I was writing about. I had been trawling through old National Geographic magazines from that time, found for me by Rony in a second-hand shop, and surfing the net researching Ugandan history. But here was someone who had actually lived through it! Of course, I asked Sheila if she would be willing to introduce me to Margaret.

By the time I was back in Scotland, Sheila had already arranged for Margaret and me to talk on the phone. Subsequently, Rony and I were invited to stay with her for a weekend in Lincoln, England.

Margaret greeted Rony and me warmly and welcomed us into her lovely home. She was so friendly and genuinely excited by what I was writing. Bits and pieces of Ugandan memorabilia were scattered around her house. The first thing she did was to scurry around collecting them and explaining each to us—table mats, stools, drums and all kinds of African utensils carved from wood. I instantly liked this generous-spirited lady.

She asked if I had a picture of my brother with me.

Of course I did, a whole album of them.

Margaret took a photograph of Frankie in her hand. "Oh, he was a handsome boy. Muganda."

It was obvious I hadn't a clue what she was talking about.

"Your brother. He was Muganda. From The Kingdom of Buganda. From the Bantu tribe. I can tell by looking at his face."

I could hardly believe it. I asked Margaret to tell me more about this Kingdom of Buganda.

"Well, they had their own King, known as the Kabaka. And their Queen, known as Nnabagereka. The Buganda people were sometimes referred to as the King's Men."

My childhood daydreams of African kings and queens were coming to life in Margaret's living room! I always loved the idea that Frankie came from a land far, far away—in my head, it was always exotic. As a child I somehow missed the TV programs with immense poverty, mud huts, witch doctors and tribal rituals. Oh, there was often some teasing at school by kids asking Frankie where his grass skirt and scary mask were. But as far as I was concerned they were idiots, especially the ones who jumped around imitating a monkey or gorilla in front of him. Frankie's left hook *did* come in handy at times. Oh, how I would love to be able tell some of those nasty children from school that my brother came from royalty!

Margaret showed me some pictures of her friends in Uganda and pointed out the features of different tribes. "See, here," she pointed to an African lady. "You can tell by the shape of the nose, the head, the color of the skin that she is a Muganda lady. And the busuuti she is wearing—that is their traditional dress—usually it's reserved for high days."

Margaret dashed off upstairs and returned with a busuuti. "Here, why don't you try mine on?"

Before I knew it, I was standing there having my photograph taken in traditional African dress. If only Frankie could see me now, how amused he would be, I thought. Margaret explained that all the different tribes have their own features and garments. "Like your Scottish tartan, some have their own woven fabric—like the Kenyan Masai. See here?"

I told her when Frankie was growing up in Scotland, everyone thought all black people looked the same. There was another black boy who lived near us who was always in and out of prison or in trouble for something. Frankie often got pulled out of school—even arrested on occasion—for crimes this other black boy had committed. The police always used to say, "Well, they all look the same to us."

Over the weekend, Margaret read some of my book. She suggested I meet Miss Sheelagh Warren who was the head teacher at Gayaza High School from 1957 to 1990.

Three weeks later we were in the car, racing through yet another amber light in London. I was starting to have trouble breathing—much to Rony's amusement. It wasn't the huge scary roundabouts or the congestion on the roads that were causing my panic; it was being over an hour late for Sheelagh. By the time we hit another road block sign, Rony realized that my fear of head teachers was very, very real.

74

Sheelagh might have agreed to meet me, but she sounded very formal on the telephone and requested I bring Frankie's adoption papers. I knew she was suspicious I might be a journalist. But I was suspicious, in turn, that she hadn't left her head teacher days behind.

When we finally arrived at Sheelagh's two-story terrace cottage, I was wishing I had packed my Rescue Remedy. I'd read there was a punishment tree at Gayaza. If a teacher wanted to punish a student for doing something wrong, they would tell the student to go and stand under the punishment tree. The aim was for the girls to feel ashamed because it faced the staff room so all the teachers and visitors would know who the naughty girl was. It was said to be thorny and not a pretty tree. I checked Sheelagh's small garden, just in case she had planted an alternative to corporal punishment outside her home.

Sheelagh opened the door and I could tell she was not impressed by my lateness. She was the epitome of the old classic head teacher. However, she accepted my apology and told me I was a silly girl to have even contemplated driving from London to Farnham when I could have so easily taken a train. Once the lecture was out of the way, Sheelagh and her friend Anne treated us to a beautiful homemade lunch. Most of it was a cold buffet—she must have known we'd be late.

Over lunch, Sheelagh relaxed and talked with great passion about "her girls" at Gayaza and the struggles some of them had to endure. It is not easy for the African girl child but it was obvious Sheelagh had their backs. Gayaza was not just a school to Sheelagh—it was her home and the girls were like her daughters. Many of her girls carried the burden of broken homes, as well as the threat of witchcraft and its practices. The stigma surrounding the menstrual cycle was horrendous and although Sheelagh didn't mention it directly, especially in front of Rony, I knew some of the girls would have been subjected to female genital mutilation. The practice is *still* very ingrained in some parts of the country; despite the fact, there are recent laws in place against the practise. I knew from researching my novel; the cutting is usually performed by women themselves who see it as an honor. Failure to initiate their daughters or granddaughters in this way can result in social exclusion. Gender inequality is still rife in the country, so it's not hard to understand boys were *always* favored when it came to education. Much was expected of *any* girl given a chance at an education. She told me how the desire for education in Uganda led to an abuse of the system and how there was pressure exerted on the head teacher to admit unsuitable candidates. Mostly it related to someone in authority, or whose bribe was the biggest. She said, "It was an educational rat race."

Everywhere I looked in Sheelagh's house there were biblical quotes and pictures of Jesus. She was a missionary in Uganda for over forty years. Born there to missionary parents, she later returned and taught throughout the most turbulent post-colonial years. As far as Sheelagh was concerned, God would protect and provide for those who put their trust in him. She believed in all that happened, however fearful, God was there. Sheelagh had looked down the barrel of several guns. She lived through chaos in the country. From 1972, a regime of torture began and many professional people fled or were murdered. Sheelagh told us that even when the British Consulate ordered her to leave the country for her safety, she had snuck out of the Consulate, jumped in her car and told her driver to go back to Gayaza: she wasn't leaving her girls.

After the liberation from Idi Amin, there was a merry-go-round of presidents, followed by a raging civil war with its horrors lasting for almost ten years. Sheelagh lived through it all. Most of the killings took place in the Luweero Triangle only a few miles from Gayaza High School. Armed men crossed the compound almost daily. Every journey outside the school was a risk-taking adventure of road blocks and intimidation; water and electricity were erratic and there was no phone service. She spoke of the loss of staff and lives threatened, yet the school never closed. The children never missed a meal or an exam. In fact, Gayaza became a refuge for many who had nowhere safe to sleep. Sheelagh and Anne, who had also been a teacher at Gayaza, sometimes welled up as they recalled those days.

After lunch, the ladies pulled out photo album after photo album. They showed Rony and me pictures of her girls in their busuutis. Sheelagh claimed her school had invented the busuuti and went into an elaborate tale to back it up. "It used to be a long piece of cloth tied under the armpit until Miss Allen designed a yoke for it in 1905. You know my dear, the larger the lady looks in her busuuti the more respect she will gain. Thinness is not admired in Uganda." She said it while looking right at me. She pointed out the various colors worn by the girls and the ladies and the symbolism each had. I'd never seen so much color and pattern! She shared pictures of formal occasions where her schoolgirls would switch their immaculate white and red uniforms for tribal costumes and sing and dance with patriotic flags flying in the background. She produced a vast array of pictures of blazing flowers set against deep blue skies and faces of joy with bright smiles. Despite the harrowing tales in our earlier conversation there was no evidence of weary faces in these photographs. Only the resilience of the human spirit shone through. I felt humbled to be sitting in the company of these courageous ladies.

After much reminiscing about Gayaza, Sheelagh asked to look at the adoption papers. Suddenly Sheelagh started repetitively tapping on the piece of paper. "I know that name...that name Wevugira...I know it. I don't know why or how I know it, but I know that I know that name from Gayaza. It's a very unusual African name."

I grabbed Rony's hand. "I have goose bumps. Are you sure, Sheelagh?"

Sheelagh looked right at me. "Yes. Yes. I know that name Wevugira."

I looked away, afraid I might cry. Sheelagh could see this meant a lot to me. She patted my hand, "Just leave it with me my dear. It will come to me. My eighty-year-old brain doesn't work as well as it used to, but it will come to me in time."

There was no doubt I had been serendipitously led to both Margaret and Sheelagh. But Sheelagh couldn't remember where or who the connection was with the name and I wondered if I was once again being led on a wild goose chase.

Then, two weeks later, I received an email from Sheelagh. She'd remembered where she knew the name from and confirmed it with one of her Old Girls—another teacher at the school. She believed Frankie's grandfather to have been the pastor of her school from 1950 to 1960. I had not only placed the lead character of my novel at that school, but now I had discovered that Frankie's grandfather worked there. I couldn't believe it—now I *had* to go to Gayaza.

Long-Lost Family

Gayaza High School
Uganda, 2012

As I think about Sheelagh and all the memories she shared with me about her turbulent post-colonial years at Gayaza, I can't help but survey the room looking for bullet holes. In 1988, when Princess Anne visited the school, Sheelagh wondered where best to seat her in case she became distracted by the number of bullet holes in the wall.

I point to a picture behind a Dickensian-looking desk strewn with paperwork, "Wow, look Rony; it's Sheelagh."

Vicky looks surprised. "You know our Sheelagh?"

"Yes. I met with her at her home in Farnham, England. She is one of the reasons I'm here."

"Oh, wow. God is good. I am an Old Girl of Gayaza. Joined in 1973. We girls of that year call ourselves 'the firstborn' of Sheelagh Warren."

Sheelagh has left such a powerful legacy; I can feel her presence in the room as surely as if she is standing here. I want to ask where the bullet holes are but our tea has arrived. We sit down around the small table at the front of the room. A gentle breeze pushes through the open slats of the window and I'm grateful for it.

I explain to Vicky I had an adopted brother whose parents were Ugandan. I tell her I know very little about his mother but, by a very strange coincidence, I met Sheelagh Warren just months before I was coming to Uganda and she thinks perhaps my brother's grandfather was the pastor of the school from 1950 to 1960.

Vicky just about leaps from her chair. She lifts her hands and places them in a prayer position, "Oh, praise the Lord," she says with vigor. "Praise the Lord indeed." She brings her hands back down and places them firmly on my lap, leaning into me until we're almost nose to nose. "And Sheelagh remembers this man?"

"Yes," I say. "It would seem so."

"And now you are here! Here at Gayaza." She throws her hands wide. "All the way from Scotland." She lifts up her hands again. "This is a sign from God." She pats my lap again and looks at me. "We must find him."

"Oh," I say, "that would be good." *Find him, find Frankie's grandfather? The guy is surely dead. He's probably been dead for 50 years. If he were alive, he'd be over a hundred years old and that would indeed be a miracle.*

I put my cup of tea down. "I had wondered if perhaps there is a photograph of Pastor Wevugira somewhere or perhaps the church he preached in is still standing. I know it was a *long* time ago." I emphasize the word long, just in case she's missed something.

Vicky leans in again, this time doing a kind of break-dance move with her head. "Did you say Wevugira?"

"Yes. I think that's how you pronounce it."

Vicky repeats the name again and again, "Wevugira. Wevugira. Wevugira."

By now I have noticed that Ugandans do like to re-peat themselves, and often repeat what you have just said. But I'm thinking maybe it's my pronunciation that has got her looking so quizzical.

It seems to me there are two types of Ugandans. There are the Ugandans that hardly move a facial mus-cle when they talk and who sit back patiently when someone else is talking. And then there is the type that has these amazing facial and body expressions. They seem to somehow throw their whole body into a con-versation, their faces contracting and contorting with every sentence. Vicky, it has to be said, falls into the latter category.

She puts her hand on my lap again and pushes in closer, "Wevugira." Vicky stares right at me. "I know that name! Why do I know that name?" She shakes her finger like the head teacher she is. "That name came up in conversation the other day. Now let me think, let me think." She looks up at the ceiling as if it holds the answer. Even the oscillating fan seems to be whispering, "Wevugira, Wevugira."

I'm starting to think that this name has a connection to some long-forgotten witch doctor's spell that makes everyone think they know it. There is movement outside the office. Vicky stands up like a meerkat and looks outside. "Phibi! Phibi! Come into my office."

A middle-aged African lady walks up the short, paved path leading to Vicky's office. The door is open to greet her. She is dressed in classic African attire: a swirl of orange and brown patterned skirt and top clinging neatly to her curvy physique.

"Ah, Phibi. I did not expect to see you today. Please, meet my new friends from Scotland."

Phibi stands back a little with her hands clasped in front of her stomach, head tilted to the side. She smiles broadly. "Ah, Scotland. Welcome. Welcome to Uganda."

"Phibi. I think you know something about the Wevugiras? Did you not say something to me about the Wevugiras just the other day?"

"Yes. Yes, Janet. She's in the cupboard."

"In the cupboard?"

"Yes. Yes, the big cupboard. The one behind your desk. We had a hard time opening it, but Janet is in there."

Rony and I look at each other. Surely Frankie's mum is not in that big old cupboard facing me. I mean things were getting strange but still!

"Sorry," I say to Phibi. "Do you mean there is something about Janet Wevugira in that cupboard?"

"Yes, my dear. I found an old photograph of Janet in there just the other day. You see, I did not know until the other day that Janet had actually attended this school as a young girl. I only noted it because well—" Phibi sees the tears falling from my face and asks, "Why are you so upset my dear?"

Frankie's mum

I am hardly able to talk for the tears streaming down my face into my mouth. I mumble, "Janet Wevugira was my brother's mother."

It is as if the Ugandan rains have stopped. The only thing making a sound is the hypnotic fan still whispering *Wevugira, Wevugira.* Finally, the chattering birds outside the open windows give me permission to break the silence. And it's my turn to start chattering away. Before I know it, I have told them the *whole* story. Ugandans like stories. They listen in like children—*oohing* and *aahing* and twisting their faces, opening and closing their eyes, shaking their heads back and forth, reflecting the emotions they are feeling from the story.

Vicky starts rocking back and forth in her chair. "Oh, my God, Oh, my God."

Oh, dear, I'm thinking to myself. *This looks very bad. These women look traumatized by this news. What on earth have I got myself into? I should have never opened that stupid manila folder! I should have never come to Uganda or started writing my novel! I should have left the past where it belongs—in the past!*

Phibi is still standing, hands folded over her stomach, head tilted to one side. Then she tilts it to the other side, looking at me curiously. I can almost see her mind ticking over, trying to fit the pieces of this rather complicated jigsaw puzzle together. Her head does that weird break-dance head move thing that Vicky's does. "You mean she gave up her *child*. Janet. And Janet was your brother's mother? Janet Wevugira, in Scotland. She had a baby boy. And the boy *died*?" Her neck sticks out as long as she makes the last word last.

"Yes." I say it as if I am testifying in a courtroom.

Phibi's eyes are wide open, fully dilated like a shocked cartoon character. "Oh, God. Oh, God. And you are the boy's sister!"

I start crying even harder and telling them I didn't come here to open up Pandora's Box. Janet probably hadn't told anyone she had given up her child. I explain I didn't come here to find his family, I came for research for my novel. The last thing I was expecting to find was Janet in the cupboard.

Vicky jumps up, "No. No! Don't you see my dear girl; you have come here for a reason! The Lord has brought you here today. You have written this novel for a reason. The good Lord has brought you here to find this family. We will help you." Vicky raises her arms again. "Praise the Lord, this is a miracle. A real-life miracle. In this room today!"

"Praise God!" Phibi joins in the chorus. "You are right. You are so right. It's a *miracle!*" Phibi goes on to justify this miracle even more by telling us she was not supposed to be in school today. She had forgotten her paperwork and decided to come in and pick it up—just at the very time we were visiting Gayaza. She didn't know anyone would even be at the school since it was a holiday.

The two women are practically singing in unison, "Oh, God is good! Oh, praise God. God *is* good *indeed!*" In fact, now they are dancing. They are doing the Bugandan Shuffle, as I have come to call it endearingly. It's a hip-swinging Ugandan happy dance. I swear they are also tongue trilling.

I want to join in the dance. It's hard to stay still, but my head is pounding and I have one hundred and one questions and apprehensions running through my head right now.

Phibi notices I've withdrawn. She tilts her head to the side again and looks at me sympathetically. "You look so worried my dear. Do not worry. I know the family. I am a relative. Phibi, me, I will help you find your family."

Oh, no. A relative. Please, God help me. I am sorry I opened that folder. Janet is going to be furious that I have told her secret. She's probably moved on, and here I am all these years later showing up in Uganda asking her to relive the pain, the shame! Oh, good God, what have I done? But no, maybe I'll be able to speak to Janet in private and tell her what a wonderful life Frankie had, what an amazing brother I had. Maybe Janet needs to know what happened to her son and that's why all this has happened. I convince myself God really did want me to come here and find Frankie's mother and show her pictures of her son and tell her all about his childhood. *But no. Oh no. How do I tell her that he died? Oh, God, this is a mess!*

Vicky puts her hand on my lap again. "It's okay, dear. Please don't worry. Know that I am here for you also."

I finally ask the question I have been aching to ask. "Is Janet still alive?"

Phibi tilts her head to the side, closes her eyes for a moment and then says softly, "No, my dear. Janet died some time ago now." She sees the tears covering my face again and says, as if in comfort, "But she had three boys that are still alive. My dear, you have brothers! Let me call Frank. We must speak to Frank."

"Frank!" Rony and I say in unison.

"Yes, Frank is the eldest brother."

I mumble through my trembling lips, "That was my brother's name."

Rony puts his arm around me. He has been filming some of the day's events but has long since stopped. "Maybe you should let Phibi call Frank. They are right. You've been brought here for a reason, Michaela. He even has the same name." He reminds me of my belief in the universe. "When you're doing the right things, the right things happen." Even Rony is starting to believe that the universe has set up this coincidental meeting.

But I insist, "No! How could I tell these boys their mother gave up a child for adoption in Scotland? I am sure she hasn't told anyone."

"My dear, what can we do to help you?" Phibi asks.

Vicki puts her hand on my lap again, "We know Janet did the right thing. It was the only thing she could have done. She could never have come back to Uganda with an illegitimate child. It is okay. We understand only too well her situation. Things have changed since then. We understand. No one will judge her harshly. She did the best thing for her child."

They are so nice to me. These two complete strangers. They are genuinely moved by my story and want to help me. I agree it is all very strange. I always knew I'd come to Uganda; even as a child, I dreamt about Africa. But this is beyond even my imagination.

I whimper, "If I could just see a picture of her, please? I've never seen a picture of his mum."

Well, Phibi was not exaggerating when she said the big old cupboard was hard to open. After all this, it seems as if Janet doesn't want to give herself up. It takes three men and a couple of tools to eventually pry the cupboard open. By this point, I am hoping there is also a bottle of brandy in there.

Phibi reaches in and pulls out a large black photograph album. As she does so, she explains that the other day she was asked to compile an album of some of the Old Girls. That was when she had come across the picture of Janet.

We flick through the photograph album. My heart is literally in my mouth. To see a picture of Janet is beyond my wildest expectations. I don't believe anyone could be more excited if it were their own biological mother they were going to see a picture of for the first time.

Janet is absolutely beautiful and Frankie's double! Dressed in white, with small pearls around her neck, she looks like the epitome of innocence. The photograph is dated 1946-1948. There is no doubt this is Janet, my brother's mother. I hold the picture in my hand. *Hello, Janet,* I say to myself. *It's nice to finally put a face to your name. Did you know I used to wonder about you? Did you guide my journey? Or was it Frankie?* The tears fall hard again as I imagine them both with us, right at this very moment.

"Michaela, you should let me call Frank. He's your brother now and I am their Auntie Phibi."

"You're their *aunt*?"

"Yes, my dear. Frankie's grandmother is still alive. She's my mum's sister. So they call me Auntie."

"You mean Janet's mother is still alive?" *Oh, no this is all too close for comfort. I could happily stop at the picture of Janet, but the fact that Phibi is a relative and a not-so-distant one is just too weird for words. And his grandmother—alive—how is that even possible?*

"Phibi," I said. "Think about it. How on earth do I tell an old lady her daughter got pregnant during her studies in the UK and gave up the baby for adoption? There is no way I could EVER do that."

"No, no, she's not her *real* mother, but she accepted Janet as her own. Pastor Wevugira's first wife died and he remarried. That girl was my mother's sister, and she is the grandmother of your family. Let me call Frank for you. I won't say anything. You can talk to Frank. Trust us. God has brought you here."

I admit there are more coincidences flying around the room than mosquitoes. The Scot in me is saying to myself that it's time for the pub; everything gets fixed in the pub over a wee drink. Only this is a high school for girls and the strongest thing around is a Coca-Cola. Of course, Ugandans think Coca-Cola fixes everything—even amoebic dysentery, as I have discovered. Anyway, I am not allowed the decision or a Coca-Cola because the next thing I know Phibi is on the phone talking to someone in Luganda. She passes me the phone.

"Hello, this is Frank; I understand you knew my mum when she was in Scotland and have some information to share?"

"Eh, yes." *What am I saying, I knew her? I don't know her or anything about her other than the fact that she gave up a son, my brother, your brother. I have obviously never met her. What on earth has Phibi said to him?*

"That is good. I will be happy to meet you today."

"Today!"

"Yes. Let us meet today. Where are you staying?"

I tell him and he says, "Perfect. I shall be there at two p.m. Is that okay?"

"Yes."

"Good." And he hangs up. No goodbyes. Nothing else. Ugandans don't say goodbye on the phone; they just hang up.

I ask Phibi another burning question. "What age is Frank?"

Phibi tells me she thinks he is in his early fifties, which would make him older than Frankie and me. But that isn't the picture I have in my head of Janet as an innocent young girl being led astray by some medical student. This means Frank was born before Frankie. But Janet wasn't married. At least, she had told the adoption agency she wasn't married. What is the real truth? If she was married before she went to the UK and had an affair, I am about to meet her eldest son. What on earth will I say to him?

Hoarding

Scotland, 1971

During the night, Frankie stole food. He was too small to reach the cupboard shelves but he knew to get the stool and climb up. He hoarded it in his blankets, under the pillows and the sheets. It upset Mum. His squirreling made crumbs in the bed. It didn't matter however many times Mum told him there was enough food to eat, he still got up during the night, stole whatever he could find, and hid it in his bed.

I wish I'd never asked for my Santa sweeties that day. I'd been looking forward to eating them as they were so colorful, a rainbow of colors. Some twisted, some wrapped, some soft, some hard, some gummy. Love Hearts, Fizzers, Refreshers all fought for my attention. When Santa gave us each a bulk bag, my five-year-old excitement was hard to contain. I can still remember Frankie and me looking into each other's bag to see if we had different sweeties and if one of us had more than the other. Mum suggested she put them away so we could enjoy them over a period of time; the last thing she needed while she was studying was two sugar-crazed kids running around.

Our first Christmas together

One day I asked Mum if I could have my bag down from the shelf. Since I had been such a good girl, she obliged. Guess what? The bag was missing and the sweetie wrappers were under Frankie's bed. Oh, I wish I hadn't cried. But I was five years old. I'd never seen so many sweeties in my life and my brother had eaten them all.

Of course, Frankie denied it and denied it and Mum got angrier and angrier. It ended with his bottom getting slapped, or as we say in Scotland—his bahookie got skelped. (Parents did that in those days without fear of condemnation.) Of course, Frankie getting a skelp made me cry even harder. I felt so guilty—I told Mum I didn't care about the sweeties, but it was too late.

Mum was frustrated by the whole situation. It didn't matter how many times she told Frankie he could have what he wanted, that he didn't need to get up in the night and steal food and hoard it, he still did it.

Many years later, Mum and I were snuggled in bed one night at the Marie Curie Hospice. I was on the cot bed beside her. Our roles in life had changed by then and I was now her primary caregiver. She told me one time she'd wondered if she just let Frankie eat everything and anything he wanted then it might help him to feel more secure. So, she did just that and Frankie ate and ate and ate till he was sick. She told me how awful she felt for doing that to him, but she thought she'd be showing him that he didn't have to worry about never having enough food to eat. I can understand. Sadly, it didn't seem to cure Frankie of his hoarding. But what might be worse was that Mum was still holding on to the guilt of that little experiment in her last days. And I'm still holding on to the guilt of the Santa sweeties.

There were two more letters that I found in the manila folder which might explain some of Frankie's behavior.

In 1979, Dad contacted the Church of Scotland Committee of Social Responsibility to ask for more details about Frankie's adoption. The reply stated:

Francis was placed in the Children's Home directly from hospital and had at no time been introduced to a foster family. This, unfortunately, leaves a gap in his early life.

Then a further letter, dated only a few months later, from the same lady, contradicting that statement:

Although there is not a great deal of information relating to Frankie's background history, I would be only too willing to pass this information to you for future use. I feel it would be helpful for us to meet and discuss the advisability of passing on this type of information and any further matters relating to the adoption and if it is convenient, I suggest we meet Wednesday, April 11 at 2:00 p.m.

Although there is no written evidence of the meeting between my father and this social worker, I know what that gap in Frankie's life was—a painful gap that Frankie probably never knew about. From her bed at the hospice, Mum told me Frankie was previously fostered with the view to adopt and then sent back to the children's home. A double whammy!

From the contradiction in the letters, the information about Frankie's first placement seems to have been covered up initially. Perhaps it was to protect Frankie emotionally, or perhaps it was in case it put off any other potential adoptive parents.

It wasn't that Frankie had been a bad child, Mum assured me. It was that the young couple who wanted to adopt him came up against so much racial prejudice from their relatives that they eventually found the adoption impossible. The parents of the couple wishing to adopt Frankie told them that they would disown them if they went ahead with it. And so, Frankie was sent back. No wonder he hoarded his food. No wonder he wet the bed. No wonder he didn't cry at night. No wonder, no wonder, no wonder.

I can only imagine Frankie's young mind, thinking that at any time these people who were looking after him could disappear without notice. Even though he was cared for in the same way as I was, he must still have held on to that underlying fear of abandonment. My parents never told Frankie he had been sent back to the children's home in his early life. I think it was just as well. But I am sure he knew, subconsciously.

Mum told me she thought she was having a nervous breakdown during those early years. It can't have been easy. She was a young mother, trying to improve her lot for herself and her family by studying to become a nurse. My father was deep into his theological studies at university by day and working in a garage by night to make ends meet. The initial joy of adopting a little black boy was proving to be a strain on the family.

Today my parents wouldn't have been allowed to adopt. First, truth be told, Dad had a petty criminal past. Second, they were both poor students with two other children. But times were different then and my parents were grateful they were not subjected to the rigmarole hopeful adoptive parents have to go through today. It was perhaps a time when people were judged more on instinct than box ticking. Whoever was responsible for allowing my parents to adopt Frankie did the right thing. Regardless of the struggles my parents had, they never regretted their decision to adopt Frankie—no matter what, they loved him as their own.

CHAPTER FOUR
Kampala Time

Uganda, 2012

Gayaza is only forty-five kilometers from Kampala. However, it has become clear that it could take us hours to get through the traffic-infested capital. It's an absolute nightmare sharing the road with the crazy drivers of motorbikes called boda bodas; local taxis, called mutatus, that cram people inside like battery chickens; and some cars that are, frankly, unfit for the road. We seem to be coming across at least one breakdown every few kilometers. I decide I might as well chill and enjoy the goods on offer outside my window.

All the windows are down. There is no air conditioning in the car. I can feel the sweat on my neck start running down my back. I wish myself in the Toyota Land Cruiser that pulls up alongside us. The disparity of cars on the road is a clear reflection of the ever-widening gap between the haves and the have-nots in this country. The signage on this trendy Land Cruiser reads, 'Ugandan Health Service supported by UNICEF'. I've started to notice that the majority of brand-new four-wheel drive vehicles are the property of well-known international charities.

Street vendors mass as we sit in the traffic jam. I'm offered everything from loo rolls to live geese, anatomy charts, jump leads, dubious food, and an array of newspapers and magazines.

I look ahead and see fridges and coffins being transported on motorcycles. I even see a cow transported on one! I swear boda boda drivers believe that driving in the middle of the road is their right. The cacophony of loud electronic beats is starting to do my head in. A child street beggar orbits our vehicle, hoping to catch our attention. She looks to be around seven. I struggle with the sight of her twisted limbs and the malnourished baby she carries, even though I know she has been strategically placed to catch the attention of us travelers. I am convinced that a number of these infants are deliberately mutilated, enough to attract sympathy but not enough to be a physical burden to the parents or the putative guardian. As our car slows to a stop again, tiny, dusty hands fight for my attention, reaching in through any opening they can find. She tries to extract money from us in any way she can. She's a professional.

Her sullen eyes stare at us. "Please, please, I beg you, please help me, Miss. Please." Her beseeching manner ensures that Rony puts some small change in her pitiful little hand. Of course, I know it is probably going to go right into the hand of her "guardian" waiting across the street; the Ugandan equivalent of Dickens' Fagin. I see one little victim collapsed on the street—she probably hasn't had any food or water in this scorching heat. I offer my water bottle to the young girl still leaning on our vehicle. Our driver tells us not to encourage her and suggests we roll up our windows. These children are banners that remind me of just how desperate life is for many Ugandans.

As we carry on weaving through a gridlock of noise, pollution and smog, the potholes make me think the city must have suffered a recent military bombardment. I would roll my window back down but the terrible drainage which has backed up from last night's rains makes the smell close to unbearable.

Ahead, a car drives over the roundabout. Someone needs to tell Ugandans—as well as the stray cattle, sheep, and goats—that they are supposed to drive *around* them. It's positively entertaining—but I'm in a hurry to meet my adopted brother's brother for the first time in my life and now a boda boda driver is trying to squeeze past us with a large coffin tied to its side.

Our driver tells me to relax. "No one is ever on time in Kampala, Miss Michaela. This traffic is always terrible here. Jam, after jam. Just stay cool. Richard will get you there—soon."

I'm learning in Uganda the word *soon* can mean hours. I'm also starting to realize Ugandans love to complain about the traffic. However, I'm not convinced anyone in Kampala actually *wants* the roads to improve. First of all, it gives everyone an excuse to be late for everything, and if the traffic actually moved then how would all these street vendors and beggars survive? It also appears to give the local traffic police a chance to survey the cars for any "damage."

Richard rolls down his window, "Yes, officer."

"I see one of your brake lights is not working. That is very naughty. Very naughty indeed."

"Yes, sir, we are in a hurry, sir. I will get it fixed."

"Yes, well I am very thirsty." He strokes his AK47.

Rony leans over and hands him a bottle of coke.

"Thank you, my friend. You are very smart, but your driver here is not so smart. I must charge him for this offense." He takes out his notebook and slowly searches for a pen.

Richard whispers to Rony, "Have you got some dollars on you?"

"How much?"

"Just a few should do."

Richard hands the officer ten dollars.

"Ah. Thank you. I see your muzungu friend has saved you from a ticket. He is very smart." He hits the side of the car and sends us on our way.

It seems these angelically-dressed police officers who marshal the traffic make sure everything is running as smoothly as the lining of their pockets.

Richards laughs. "He spied you. The muzungu tourists. The car beside me might not have a windshield, and it might be blowing black smoke from its exhaust, but if they see a muzungu in my car, they will try to fine me by finding any flimsy excuse."

Uganda is riddled with corrupt tendering processes, and it seems even traffic jams add to the Black Economy.

Finding a New Brother

We finally arrive at our guest house. I've got about five minutes to make myself look somewhat presentable. Oh, my God, what the heck do I wear to meet my brother's brother?

I yell at Rony, "My hair's a mess! Look at me!" I reach into the suitcase and bring out my portable heated rollers. Okay, give me a break, folks —it was my first time in Uganda. They have never come with me again! First, it is far too hot to contemplate them next to your head and second, the security guards at the airport think they are some kind of bomb or new form of ammunition for a machine gun. Take my advice; if you don't want to be hauled away and almost miss your plane then do not take heated rollers to Uganda. Still, in my panic to look good for my new brother I plug them in.

"What will I wear? Don't just stand there, Rony. Help me!" I'm having a meltdown. Poor Rony pulls out a nice white lace dress.

"No, it's too short. Ugandans don't like women to wear short clothes. He's probably a strict Christian. After all, his grandfather was a pastor."

Another outfit.

"Nope, it's too pale. Ugandans like color."

Another outfit.

"I read that Ugandans don't like women in trousers; they prefer skirts and dresses."

Rony is thankful that I have traveled light and therefore have little choice. "What's wrong with what you're already wearing?" He asks.

It's a bright ankle-length dress. He is right. It is perfect.

There is not much point in doing my hair in Uganda. It's hot and humid and putting on makeup makes even less sense. Still I have to try, after all; it's not every day I meet my brother's brother for the first time in my life.

Our guest house sits on the slopes of Namirembe Hill. It might command a million-dollar view but you wouldn't have paid a single dollar for the first room we were offered. Only if you were some kind of religious fanatic on some kind of penance would you have wished to stay in that room; the plastic basin in the middle of the floor and the two small twin beds gave it a cell-like quality. They had just discovered upon registration that we weren't married! Shock, horror and unspoken condemnation of our sinful ways is what I think led them to offer us that dark, lonely room at the end of the corridor.

Rony declined 'The Mandela Suite,' as he called it and after some monetary negotiations we were moved to something better. The room I'm now getting ready in at least has a double bed and a shower rather than a bucket.

We have arranged to meet Frank in the small dining area outside. It is surrounded by lovely plants and shrubs, but is basic in both its food and its décor. The hot-food trays are still laid out, but they are empty other than one that has a shin bone complete with kneecap and hoof hanging out of it.

I'm sitting on a white plastic chair, slowly melting into it and wishing we had picked somewhere better.

Our guest house is a Christian establishment and therefore does not serve alcohol. Perhaps it's a good thing I can't order a large brandy as my emotions are already heightened, but boy am I ready for a glass of something stronger than African tea. My heart is racing. I'm filled with a sense of conflict and anxiety.

Lots of men appear in Frank's age group, many wearing church garments: purple, black, white, and gold all parade the stairs of the guest house. White pastoral collars and gold crosses fight for my attention. Each of these men looks right at me—probably because I am looking right at them. I wonder if Frank has taken after his grandfather and become a pastor. I'm sorry I didn't ask that question back at Gayaza.

Ugandans always greet muzungus. I'm fooled into believing they are all Frank. I even pick out the ones with long embroidered African dress—perhaps Frank, like me, wanted to dress up for the occasion. Then a man appears at the top of the stairs wearing a yellow and brown-checked shirt and beige trousers. He's carrying a black briefcase and white plastic bag under his arm. There is no doubt this is Frank. He looks so like Frankie that it takes my breath away. I bolt upright from the chair. We are easy to spot, the only muzungus there. Frank comes toward our table. I can't speak. Tears have started.

Frank doesn't understand why this strange white woman is crying all over him. I want to compose myself but he looks so like Frankie that it's simply impossible for me not to cry. I feel this unimaginable link and want to give Frank the biggest hug in the world, but he knows *nothing* about why I'm here.

We all sit down at the stark white table. Frank instinctively takes my hand and keeps hold of it. I'm thinking, *this is totally surreal. I'm holding hands with Frankie's brother in Uganda. This morning I didn't even know he existed! I can't stop staring at him. My God, he even wrinkles his nose the same way as Frankie when he smiles.* We just sit there until I can compose myself. I don't know where or how to start.

Eventually Frank takes the lead. "Did you know my mum well?"

"No," I sniffle. "I didn't know your mum at all. I knew your brother."

"My brother?" He looks quizzically at me.

"Yes. You had a brother who was my brother in Scotland."

"Oh." He speaks very calmly. "That was where my mum was a student."

"Well, Northern Ireland actually. She studied in Belfast. It's near Scotland."

"Oh, right. I can't believe it. And my mum had a baby there. A baby boy."

"Yes, she did. And he was my brother. My parents adopted him into our family as an infant."

Frank looks at me for a long moment and says nothing. Then his eyes enlarge. "Wow. I don't know what to say." He reaches his hands over his head and leans back in the chair. "Oh, God. Oh, God. This is totally amazing. I can hardly believe it."

"It's true, Frank."

"I believe you. But, wow, this is amazing. Totally amazing. Is he here with you?" He looks around, moving his head from side to side as if expecting Frankie to be standing close by. "When can I see him?"

It is gut-wrenching to have to tell Frank his brother is dead. He wants to know how and why. He wants all the details. I hate explaining—I hate remembering. Frank takes it stoically. My aching sense of loss isn't the same for Frank. How could it be? Frankie is a complete stranger to him.

"Wow," he repeats. "Then all this makes you my sister. I always wanted a sister. This is unbelievable! Let me give you a hug." Frank hugs me and hugs me till I can barely breathe.

Wow, I'm thinking. *He's taken this really well! I have a new brother. I really do have a brother, just like my brother who died. He even looks like him. How amazing is this? I'm not an orphan anymore. I have a family again. Isn't life wonderful?*

I tell Frank everything I know about the circumstances of the adoption, and he listens intently. All he can say is *wow, wow, wow, this is amazing, truly amazing.* He's not upset or angry at this news—he's excited. But then I tell him his brother's name.

"That is *my* name. My father named me Frank. It means a man who knows his father."

Frank seems suddenly defensive and questions why his mother would choose to call a child, who was born after him, by the same name. He tells me this is not done in Uganda. I know a nerve has been hit.

I ask if he would like to see a picture of his brother. I've come to Uganda prepared; I have a small album of Frankie's life. I show him the one of Frankie wearing his kilt first.

"Oh, my God!" Frank puts his hands over his face.

100

I reach out to him and gently rub his arm.

He takes a deep breath, "Oh, my God. He looks like me!"

This is when the emotion that Frank has been keeping in finally shows and he realizes he did indeed have a brother with the same name who lived a *very* different life to his own.

His brother lived in a country where men, just like his brother in this photograph, wear tartan kilts. Where they eat something called haggis and eat fish and chips on the street. And are rich—very rich, because everyone in the United Kingdom is rich—right? Oh, this brother must have had a very good life. A very good life indeed.

I know Frank is deeply moved by the fact that he had another brother. It could have been such a different scenario. But it all seems as natural as it is astonishing for us to be together. We are two people with integral parts to play in a story that started in Belfast in 1966. Somehow, we have been miraculously brought together across continents. The conversation flows back and forth like the flock of birds above our heads. There is a natural ease, understanding, and curiosity.

Just like I want to know about his mother, he wants to know *all* about his brother: his likes, dislikes, height, weight—simply everything. And everything I say Frankie liked or was like, he says he likes or is like too.

But I have instinct enough to know this is not really the case. I also have the instinct to know he is upset about their name being the same; he keeps asking why his mother would do that. I also sense that as Frank looks at the pictures of Frankie's childhood, Frank is thinking his brother Frankie is the lucky one. After all, he got to grow up in the United Kingdom where no one was suffering the reign of Idi Amin and a raging civil war.

How can I tell him I believe that, given a choice, Frankie would have probably rather stayed in the arms of his mother than have had his heart torn apart by the separation? Frankie had his own battles in life.

I'm not lying when I tell Frank that Frankie was an extremely happy boy—always laughing and smiling—because he was. That's what made him so easy to love. But the hole that was left by the separation from his mother was a dark, lonely place, a terrifying abyss in his heart of which few were aware, as were his complexities and contradictions.

Frank has brought many photographs of his mother, including her passport and some other legal papers. Before he came he obviously took time to sift through an assortment of pictures to give an overview of Janet through the years. He has also brought pictures of his brothers: David, Paul and—wait for it—the first born in the family, Stephen. The same name and spelling as my own eldest brother. Sadly, Frank tells me his brother Stephen, his wife and children all died of AIDS.

I ask Frank why he brought all these pictures and how he knew to bring so many and so much information.

That's when Frank admits to me the family had been told their mother had given up a baby for adoption. He tells me a cousin told them about twelve years ago, but he didn't want to believe his mother could have done such a thing and thought the cousin was lying.

As I suspected, Janet never forgot about the baby she had given up; she thought about him until the day she died. It turns out Janet told her sisters that when she died, she wanted the brothers told they had another brother in the UK somewhere.

After her death, the sisters decided not to tell the boys. However, when the last aunt was on her deathbed she did tell her daughter, who was in London at the time, so she could tell the brothers the truth. She did as her mother requested, but only to Paul, who happened to be home in the UK, where he lived at the time. He managed to speak to the dying aunt on the phone and believed her. Frank told me Paul went on a one-man crusade to try and find their long-lost brother. However, without any name or paperwork, it was impossible.

Then, twelve years later, I show up out of the blue and put some of the pieces of the jigsaw puzzle together. Was I meant to go to Uganda and meet this family or what?

Frank shows me some pictures of his mum, Janet. He asks if Frankie had a gap in his teeth and points to his. "No," I say, but then I recall he had braces for a short time as a child. He hands me another picture and points to a gap in Janet's teeth. My God, I can't believe it. I called a character in my book Janet Wevugira as a kind of hidden nod to the real Janet. She is not a main character, but I gave her a gap in her teeth! How was that even possible? I can hardly comprehend it, but it makes me realize we are all *much* more connected than we think.

Frank shows me another picture of his mother and tells me it was taken not long before she died. When I ask what she died of, he looks vaguely perturbed. He takes a few moments and says, "Malaria. It was Malaria." I'm somehow not sure I believe him, but I accept his answer. I ask Frank what year she died. He tells me she died in October 1993. I almost burst out crying again. It turns out Janet died only a few months before Frankie. You see, when Frankie died I used to say to people that perhaps his mother had died and wanted him back. It was a way for me to justify the fact that his life had been cut so short and my own heart broken by the loss.

It gives me a kind of solace to think of them together again, back in each other's arms where they belong.

I believe the pull was so strong, even from the grave. My time with Frankie was short, but his mother's had been shorter. Call me a mystic dreamer, but the thought that they are reunited in some way helps my grieving process.

Frankie and me sitting on my parents bed in
Bank St, Glasgow

Twins – When One Dies, So Does the Other

Canada, 1994

There is nothing hazy about this memory.

I wake up. Someone is in the bedroom with me. Over me. They touch me. *I'm going to be murdered.* I freeze under the blankets. I can just make out the luminous green lights on the alarm clock. It reads, 1:20 a.m. I close my eyes, terrified, and pray. *Oh, God, please don't let this person kill me.* I'm convinced I'm going to die.

Someone is in this room with me. I'm not alone. I continue to pray. *Please, God. Please don't let this person hurt me.* I know someone is standing right beside me.

Next thing I know, I'm being woken by my husband, Gerry. He's a firefighter and has just come home from night shift.

"Oh, my God, I'm alive."

"Yes. You are," Gerry laughs.

"Someone was in here last night. In this room with me! I thought they were going to murder me."

"Don't be silly—the doors are locked. You were dreaming."

"No, I wasn't. I swear—it was real! Check the garage. Someone was in our house during the night."

"I'll check, but no one's been in here. You've had a nightmare."

Gerry checks the garage doors and locks and confirms that no one could have come in or out. The phone rings when Gerry is in the shower. I answer. It's the chief of the fire department. He asks if Gerry can call him back. Gerry says he'll call him after he's dropped me off at work.

A short time later, Gerry is back at my work accompanied by his sister. They're there to tell me Frankie died in a house fire the night before. I go into shock. I run around the small boutique floor—run, run, running, in and out the chrome rails as if I can run away from what I've just been told. I eventually stop and hold onto a rail and wail. It's a deep wail, primordial. I can hardly fathom where this guttural sound comes from or that I make it. Gerry catches me before I fall. After a horrendous Canadian winter journey to try to get from Ottawa to Glasgow via Montreal, I get off the plane at Glasgow and my body gives in. I'm home now. It's real. Frankie won't be here. I collapse. I can hear people over me trying to stir me, but I don't want to come around. I want to lie here and die too. When one twin dies, so does the other. I moan. I growl from the pit of my stomach. It hurts. It is agony and only dying myself will release the terror of the grief I know I will have to face. But I can't move. I don't want to move. I drift off somewhere for a time. I don't know how long. I hear Gerry. He's there. He's holding me begging me softly to come around. He keeps repeating my name, "Michaela. Michaela. It's all right. Michaela." But it's not all right. Frankie has died. Never, ever again, in my life will I get to see my brother.

Gerry was told Frankie died around 6:00 a.m. UK time. The clocks are five hours behind in Canada—the alarm clock read 1:20 a.m. when I was so oddly awoken the night before. When I finally come around, through my tears, I tell Gerry the person with me in the room was Frankie.

To this day I still feel sure that when Frankie died his spirit came to my room to be with me, to try to say goodbye. I believe he leaned over me and touched me. Gerry often testifies I told him someone was with me in my room that night and how I made him check the locks, windows and doors that freezing cold morning, February 26, 1994.

It had been an accident. It was the coldest night of the year. Frankie came in from a Friday night drinking in the pub and lay down on the sofa, the electric bar heater beside him. This style of heater was popular in Scotland for many years, giving instant heat. That night there was a rare power failure. We can only ever guess at the exact truth of the details, but reckon that Frankie thought the heater was in the off position. Unfortunately, when the power came back on during the night, so did the small heater. It smoldered away until the inevitable happened.

When I was told how it happened, all I could think about was his beautiful face. The thought that he was physically hurt, haunted me. My father told me when he went to identify his body there was not a mark on him, that it was the smoke that had killed him and he looked peaceful. To this day I am not sure if my dad was just trying to make things that bit easier for me. Gerry, as a firefighter, told me the same thing. Visiting his flat afterwards, it was hard to believe he was rescued unscathed, but I hope so. I was also grateful that my father had the careful consideration to call the chief of the fire department in Ottawa that morning and make sure I wasn't alone when I received the news.

CHAPTER FIVE

Frankie, do you remember me?

Uganda, 2012

My heart aches when I see the little Ugandans at the first Babies' Home I visit. I sense the complete and utter fear that grip the heart of every single one of these orphaned children. Babies are totally helpless and at the mercy of adults; they cannot survive without care.

Their tiny, dusty hands clutch hard to my fingers, my hair, my legs—whatever they can clutch of my anatomy. I feel like a human climbing apparatus. They need to be held. It is as necessary for them as breathing. They fight each other to be held and touched, and their hugs are as hard on my body as they are in my heart. I can't let go. Any one of them could have been Frankie and I find myself becoming more and more drawn in. I need to do something—anything—to help.

Many of the babies were abandoned under terrible circumstances. Left on the side of the road, in bushes, pit latrines, police stations and churches. They are lucky to have survived. One of the first little girls I hold was found in a plastic bag with her umbilical cord still dangling. A dog had gotten into the bag and mauled her; she was covered in maggots. Somehow, she survived, only to be diagnosed as HIV positive. No doubt this little soul was the result of rape or prostitution; both are prevalent in Uganda. I cried when I heard an American couple adopted her a year later. There is a good side to adoption, a very good side.

Kampala, Uganda, volunteering with some orphaned infants

As I walk the narrow corridor, tiny grasping, needy fingers reach out from the metal bars of the deteriorated cot beds. It is as if I can hear them plead, "Please, Mummy. Come and get me. I'll be good, Mummy. I promise." "Pick me. Pick me. I'll be good. I promise." They *all* need and want a mummy. To be loved is their human right!

I think of Mum and Dad. Was this how they felt when they went to Tanker Ha' Children's Home and saw the children there? If it was, then no wonder they didn't think twice about the color of Frankie's skin. I'm not sure what they would have done if they had ever come to Uganda. I imagine I might have had a lot more brothers and sisters. I remember Dad telling me he'd have taken every single one of the children from Tanker Ha' home if he could. Mum also told me, when she was in the Marie Curie Hospice, that she had later wished she had adopted at least one more child. Despite the difficulties, she said it had all been worth it.

Before I left to come here, I decided to organize a baby shower for Ugandan orphans. We held it at my friend Eta Leslie's home and, with the help of family, friends, and Christina Manca's filming of the event, we raised just over £3,000. We also filled three large suitcases full of much-needed supplies and gifts for a local Babies' Home. A few of my friends were having their own babies at the time, and they couldn't even begin to use most of the things gifted to them at their baby showers. Our unique little baby shower meant Ugandan babies benefited considerably.

It is hard to come to terms with the dichotomy. My friends who were having babies had rooms full of gifts. They had everything and more you could imagine a mother needs, yet here in Uganda these orphaned babies have absolutely nothing. Not even milk.

The money we raised manages to pay for life-saving surgery for one of the Ugandan infants. Lawrence is a lovely, wee two-year-old with a hernia the size of a coconut. When we see him the day after his surgery, we find him playing in the sandpit at the babies' home. He has a large dressing on his wound, but I still can't believe he is sitting in amongst so much dirt. In Scotland, any child post-surgery would either still be in a hospital or be at home being mollycoddled. But, other than being a bit grumpy and sore, you wouldn't have known Lawrence had just had major surgery. Rony soon has Lawrence giggling away on his lap. It is humbling to know we have helped this child and possibly saved his life.

Oh, Frankie, why are you not here with me in Uganda? Why did you have to die? We should have come here together. I can't do this alone. I can't fix the hole in the hearts of these children. I can't dry all these tears. It's overwhelming. I want to help. I need to help. God, tell me—what do you want me to do? How can I help these children?

We also discover five children have died from pneumonia at the home recently, so some of the money we raised is put toward immunizations against pneumonia. The money also helps to pay for the Home's ongoing costs. But most important to me is the day we install the fire safety equipment.

It was not a request I had been expecting, especially since the Babies' Home knew nothing about me or Frankie or how he had died. Before I left for Uganda, I sent them a short email asking what they needed most. A strange request came back for fire extinguishers. It took me by surprise that there are actually many fires in Uganda due to electrical storms and faulty wiring. Most places wired for electricity in Uganda wouldn't pass a basic safety test.

I was moved by this request and wrote back to them immediately. I told the matron of the home, I would be happy to put the fire equipment in and would like to do so in memory of my brother who died in a fire in Glasgow.

On the day we are to install the equipment we get up very early, drive across town and deposit the money required at the Fire Masters.

Now, as I said before, everyone is late in Kampala and the Fire Masters are no exception. The Fire Masters inform me they will be there by 10:00 a.m., but by 2:00 p.m. they haven't arrived and I am starving. We've been up since 6:00 a.m. and have already driven across the city and back.

Rony and I decide to take a driver to the nearest little café for a bite to eat. We tell the Babies' Home to call us the minute they arrive as we want to film the extinguishers being installed. Of course, no sooner has our egg and chips arrived but the phone rings. We wolf down the café's only answer to fast food and jump in the car.

Just as we are driving through the gates of the home and I spot the Fire Master's van, the song, "Frankie" by Sister Sledge comes on the car radio! I cannot believe it—that was Frankie's song! The song was such a hit in the early eighties and of course, we used to tease Frankie by singing it to him. The chorus goes like this:

Oh, Frankie, do you remember me?
Do you remember me? Me, Frankie.

It is as if he is saying to me, *I am right here with you, Sister and I am watching what you are doing today.*

I had spoken to him that morning. I often speak to my deceased family and friends, because as far as I'm concerned, they are not really dead; we just can't see them. I had told him what we were going to be doing that day in his memory and how much I wished he was there with me. I had asked him to give me a sign, and here it was.

All this happened the very day before I went to Gayaza High School, saw a picture of Frankie's mother and met his brother, Frank. It is easy to understand why I got the feeling that some powerful force beyond my understanding was on my side.

Everything synced up. Right down to the first dance Frank and I have together.

Modern-Day Miracles

Scotland, 2012

A month or so before we went to Uganda, Rony decided he'd had enough of his general practitioner and switched to a new doctor, a Dr. Ian Kennedy. When Rony went to see Ian for the first time at his surgery, he informed Ian he was going to Uganda and needed one more injection. Ian told him he had a very good friend, Dr. Moses Apiliga, who was from Uganda but lived in Glasgow. To Rony's surprise, right there and then Ian picked up the phone in his surgery and called Moses.

By two o'clock that same day, Rony was sitting in Moses' surgery in Scotstoun, having tea with him and explaining my story.

It turned out that Moses came to study medicine at Glasgow University in 1966, the same year Frankie was born. Just like Frankie's mother probably had been, he was unceremoniously uprooted from his home in Uganda and told he must go to the UK to study, whether he liked it or not.

You see, after Uganda gained its independence from the UK in 1962, its government sent its brightest students to the UK to study. Their tuition fees, accommodation, clothes and sometimes even a car were all paid for. In fact, as Moses stated, they felt like the richest students in Glasgow at the time.

For some Ugandans, the prospect of going to the UK to study was a dream come true. For some, like Moses, the anxiety of forced separation from his family and all he knew in Uganda caused him great upset. It was an honor and opportunity for which only a chosen few were selected, whether they wanted it or not.

Uganda was very proud and wanted its student ambassadors to present themselves well and not show the country up. Moses, like Janet, was sent on a training course, to learn how to behave in the UK. They were taught how to hold cutlery properly and other weird and wonderful things that are seemingly very *British*. One of Moses' favorite stories is that he was told he must *never* eat in the street. When he got here he couldn't believe all these people eating fish and chips out of newspaper wrappers! And poky hats—ice-cream cones—in the freezing cold weather!

He still finds it hard to eat on the street in Scotland, but not Uganda; there he loves nothing more than to stop at the street vendors who cook muchomo—long meat kebabs—on small charcoal barbeques by the side of the road. I've never tasted them as I've been advised the meat could be anything—including rat! But Moses grew up eating rat and devours these meat sticks with delight.

Needless to say, Moses and I became very good friends. If you think about the way we met, it was again, miraculous.

Before we were due to leave, Moses warned Rony and me about a few things in Uganda. He wrote them down on a sheet of paper. In fact, he thought they were so important that he wrote them down three times each.

Corruption, corruption, corruption!

Personal safety, personal safety, personal safety!

Unexpectedly, a few days before we were due to leave, Moses called and said he had to go to Uganda urgently because someone had claimed he was dead and stolen his land. We learned that this is not an unusual occurrence in Uganda, buying land there is like buying air. While this was bad news for Moses, it turned out to be great news for Rony and me. Having Moses there in person to help us navigate a complex country was wonderful, and he facilitated many things for us. But perhaps the thing I was most grateful to Moses for was the party he threw for us on the evening of the day I met Frank.

Don't Worry About a Thing

Uganda, 2012

Moses is the first person I call to tell I have found Frankie's brother. Moses says he has been praying for this miracle as he knew in his heart I wanted to find the family; he is overjoyed for me.

That evening he arranges a celebration for us all at his friend's restaurant, The Carnival. If you like meat, lots of meat, then it's *the* place to go in Kampala. You can eat as much of an assortment of meat as you want (no rat). Then, when you have finished eating, you turn a small wooden carved Gorilla on your table over onto its back.

Moses has also made sure that there is a traditional African band playing. Not only is the food an absolute feast but the traditional music and tribal dance mixed in with some more modern-day reggae are simply incredible.

Grass skirts, tribal masks, tribal makeup, creative headpieces, jewelry and spears all grace the dance floor. My childhood imagination of Africa is coming to life in front of me.

An eclectic array of traditional instruments I have never seen before are used to create this captivating music. The drums are simply hypnotic, and the speed at which these people play is incredible. The energy of the dance is worthy of an Olympic medal. The height they jump is jaw dropping. It is simply spectacular. This is Uganda at its finest, such a rich cultural heritage of stories, music and dance. All of which is on display for us as I sit with my new Ugandan brother.

When Frankie died, the album on his turntable was Bob Marley's *Exodus*. As fate would have it, the first song Frank and I dance to together at The Carnival restaurant is Bob Marley's "Three Little Birds" from that very album. It's a fantastic song that makes anyone feel better. I'm sure you know it:

Don't worry about a thing,
'Cause every little thing gonna be all right!

And at that time everything most certainly is. As soon as that song starts playing, Frank stands up and puts his hand out toward me. I know what he is thinking—I want to dance too! I can feel the rhythm in my shoulders, my legs, my heartbeat. He is grinning in that familiar way Frankie used to. As Frank walks me to the dance floor, I notice we are almost the same height. Frankie was taller than me by about four inches. The only time I was ever taller than him was when we were about six years old—and boy did I enjoy that.

Frank and I dance around the sizable wooden floor, singing along to the Bob Marley lyrics. It is as if Frankie is there in the midst of us. I'm no longer worried that I've done the wrong thing by telling people about Janet's secret. Everything is indeed *gonna be all right*. I have a new brother and my family has just expanded like the legs of the African dancer jumping in the air in front of me.

Soon everyone from our table is up dancing. Rony is grabbed by one of the dancers from the band and shown some African moves. The energy is electric.

Everyone in the room is so joyful for my coming to Uganda. Shortly after we return to the table I receive another wonderful surprise.

Frank makes a phone call from the table. "Hello Paul, you were right, the meeting was about our brother." Frank hands me the phone, "It's your brother, Paul, in the States; he wants to say hello." Paul's voice bubbles like the drink in front of me. He tells me how he had tried in vain to trace Frankie when he was living in the UK, and how disappointed he had been not to find any leads. He is quick to tell me he was the *only* one who believed the story about their mother leaving a baby boy in the UK. He explains to me he was touring with his band Limit X in Europe and he had stopped in London for a few days to visit family and friends. When he was there he called his cousin who told him her mum, his auntie, was very sick and about to pass on but she had a message from his deceased mother that she had to pass on to him. "That day, I called Auntie Pursis, her voice was weak but she told me I had a brother in the UK whom I had never met. I was in shock."

"Yes, Frank told me a bit of the story today but said, at the time, he didn't believe you."

"I didn't want to believe it either but at the same time I was asking for any contacts of my brother. She gave me some names and I promised her I would look for my brother and I would find him, and now, you show up all these years later. This is a miracle of God!"

"I know, I know. It's incredible. I can't believe I have found his family after all this time."

"I called all the hospitals and every contact I had including my mum's guardians in Belfast and no one seemed to know what I was talking about. I knew it was true and never gave up hope that God would send me my brother. Then, when Frank called today and told me he was meeting someone who knew our mum, I just knew in my heart it had to be something to do with my brother. I so want to meet him. Where is he living now?"

My heart sinks. Why has Frank not told him his brother died? I don't know what else to do but tell him the truth, "Paul, I'm not sure how to tell you this but your brother, Frankie, died a number of years ago in an accidental fire."

The excitement leaves Paul's voice and he is lost for words.

"I'm sorry, Paul. I thought Frank would have told you. All I can give you is pictures and short videos of him. I can tell you about him if you want and how he lived his short life. He was loved and had a good family."

I know Paul is sad and is finding it hard to comprehend. I sense he is genuinely upset. He tells me he so wishes he could be there with us in person to celebrate finally making contact and he is glad for that. I feel the same way.

"I cannot wait to meet you, Sister, and give you a big hug and share stories with you about our life and find out about our brother."

I tell Paul I am so happy to have found my brother's family. It has turned out to be truly one of the happiest days of my life. I have to pinch myself; here I am sitting around a table with some of Frankie's family in Uganda and with Moses' relatives. I have a new Ugandan family. Everyone is euphoric. Oh, life is good. God is good. Modern-day miracles do indeed happen.

Homing Instincts

I married a man who was adopted practically from birth—at three weeks old if I remember correctly. Gerry Foster was born in Canada, but his first set of names, given by his biological mother, was Gregory Allan Monroe—more Scottish names you could not find. As a result, Gerry had romanticized about Scotland all his life and had always wanted to visit there. When I was on holiday in Ottawa, Canada, a young red-headed girl from Scotland, was it any wonder Gerry took an interest? Being a hospitable Scot, I told him he was welcome anytime. So, Gerry arrived one day in Scotland for a holiday and four weeks later we were getting married.

I have always been drawn to people who were adopted, fostered, or who have suffered major rejection from their parents. They seem to be able to hone in on me and me on them—not just from across a room but even from across the globe. Talk about a homing instinct!

I didn't know Gerry was adopted when we first met, in Canada. He was dating a friend of mine, but the minute he found out I was Scottish I had a new best friend and she sadly lost her lover. I instinctively knew his pain. And guess what—I wanted to heal him. Did he hurt me? Of course, he did. Did I hurt him? Of course, I did.

You see, Gerry was told by his well-meaning adoptive parents that his Scottish mother loved him and was doing the very best for him by giving him up for adoption. I'm sure many adopted children are told this. It's understandable. But think about that message for a moment: *I am abandoning you because I love you.* It might have been the truth because in her heart she thought it was the best thing to do. But isn't that a bewildering statement? In my experience, it sets in motion a great deal of unconscious confusion in a person's heart between love and abandonment.

For love to be accepted there must be trust, trust that you will not be abandoned. Loving someone is scary, but I think more so for adoptees. The rejection and abandonment they fear can manifest itself in all kind of self-destructive and testing behaviors. There can often be a need to control and at times a misdirected anger at the person who loves them. That very love causes so many internal anxieties that I think, in some, it can lead to an unconscious sabotage. Love does not always conquer all—especially for the parents and lovers of adoptees.

Just like my brother, I think I have spent my life trying to calm the silent screams of the others I have loved. I wasn't qualified to do it and they weren't qualified to heal me either. But boy, was letting go of that and freeing myself from the legacy of their trauma—and mine—difficult. The hardest thing I ever did was leave Gerry. We *both* had painful lessons to learn.

Adopted children can love, oh, wow can they love! But they need to get past the subconscious anxieties. The wounds are deep and defenses are strong. Most are totally unaware of them and that makes it very tricky, sometimes dangerous, to even go there. The pain is so intense and the coping mechanisms are so ingrained. I am sure there are many adopted people out there who would say that I am wrong and this isn't the case at all for them, and they are fully adjusted human beings. But I'm taking my chances in the hopes that this might at least help the few who are not faring so well with the emotional trauma of separation.

We all want our mummies and daddies. Even if that mother beats you and puts cigarette burns on your body, often excuses are made for them and the pain internalized: you blame yourself for being a bad child. I know this because my sister-in-law, who was also adopted, was taken away from her biological mother by social services because her mother was an alcoholic. She had been found with cigarette burns on her body. Did my dear sister-in-law stop loving her mother when she found this information out? No. Instead she went in search of her biological mother as soon as her adopted mother died.

My sister-in-law left it until then as she hadn't wanted to hurt the woman who adopted her, a woman she loved dearly. Nevertheless, the need to find her biological mother was so strong that she contacted Children's Aid to search for her. She was very brave. She knew the facts but wanted—needed—to know who her mother was. She was also curious to know if she had any siblings. She felt she could not be whole until she had met her mother, and had hoped and prayed she was still alive. She did find her; she discovered her mother was also looking for her and it was a happy reunion. By that time her biological mother was a recovering alcoholic who had carried the pain of what she had done to her child with her the rest of her days. It turned out her mother lived around the corner from Gerry and me—just meters away! They were lucky to find each other; both needed to heal. It turned out Sandra did have a half-sister and they became close. Sadly, her sister died a few years later. The mother returned to alcohol shortly after, and the cycle of hurt began again. Regardless, Sandra still found solace in having found her mother and bonded with a sister. She also told me she realized that blood does not necessarily make a family.

I think most children have an unconditional love for their parents and most mothers never forget about the child they gave up for adoption. That's what makes the whole thing so tragic. Children aren't born with an ability to defend themselves from their parents, and the social systems that are in place are far from perfect. I have found this especially in the case of the ever-increasing intercultural adoption in Africa.

Me with my new brothers David and Frank

Eeenie, Meenie, Miney, Moe

Uganda, 2012

This is a big day for me. I am going to visit Janet's grave. She is laid to rest in Masaka, which is also where Frank's brother—my new brother—David lives. We have arranged to meet him in the center of Masaka town.

I feel uncomfortable using that word, "brother." Frank has taken to calling me his sister, but he is not *really* my brother. Not in the way Frankie was. I worry that I am dishonoring Frankie in some way by calling his biological siblings my brothers. Doesn't one have to earn the right to call someone a brother or a sister?

It's a pretty powerful word. Still, it seems to be the way here, so I go along with it.

Besides, I do like having this new family of brothers. It's comforting to know I have brothers, even if they don't really know anything about me. After all, my biological brother Stephen and I lived in the same house for almost sixteen years and he still doesn't know the first thing about me.

Frank has even taken to holding my hand, especially when we are crossing the streets. It's just as well as the traffic seems hell-bent on mowing me down. Crossing a busy road in Uganda is not for the faint of heart; there's a real skill to it.

We are driving approximately 170 kilometers to Masaka, but the Masaka Road is the busiest in the country and reports the highest rate of fatalities: around four hundred a year. I'm sure most of the traffic accidents could be avoided by commonsense driving but, as I am reminded on a daily basis, that doesn't exist in Uganda. The roads truly are scary and I'm still learning that nothing moves according to schedule over here.

Lush, fertile scenery hugs us from both sides of the smooth road. On the rougher roads, small villages fight for our attention, as do the children shouting, "Muzungu!" and waving excitedly at us. We wave back with just as much enthusiasm.

Bare feet and broad smiles chase the car, curious to see white faces. They are hoping we will throw them some loose change or a bottle of juice. The red dust whirls and swirls as the car rushes rapidly on, leaving small dusty figures waving off the muzungu royalty who has just driven past.

We pass ladies young and old, gracefully carrying their goods on their heads like the caryatides of Athens. Not even an earthquake could cause anything to topple from those heads. We see a young girl who looks to be around ten years old struggling with ten-liter jerry cans in each hand and a baby strapped to her back. We drive past the hungry and the thirsty. I see one young girl trying to get the dregs of juice from a bottle thrown out of a car window. She's too thirsty to chase our car. I watch her meander along till she finds another bottle and drinks what is left. I know that not far behind her will be the plastic bottle collector boys. A kilo of these discarded bottles earns them fifty cents, and it takes hundreds to make up a kilo.

The day is going well; we arrive at the equator bang on time. I get to witness the water going down the hole clockwise on the north side, anticlockwise on the south and straight down in the center.

All this science makes it a tourist attraction, so vendors are lining the street on both sides. I buy some lovely African jewelry and a few souvenirs, but decide to pass on the food. I'm learning that unless you know exactly where and how it is cooked it is better to go hungry or, if you're like me and need to eat regularly, then bring snacks with you in the car.

Another hour's drive and we will be meeting David in Masaka. David is a teacher, just like his mother. He's actually the deputy head of a government school, Kabungo Secondary School. I'm so excited to see him in the flesh. So far, I've only seen pictures of David; there is some resemblance to Frankie, around the eyes mainly, but it is not as obvious as it is with Frank. I am much more emotionally prepared meeting David than I was with Frank. However, the same can't be said about visiting Janet's grave. I want to take flowers so we have arranged to meet David just outside a market in Masaka.

I spy David immediately. He's slightly smaller than Frank. He's well-dressed, wearing a white and black checked suit jacket, black and white striped shirt and smart trousers. I know he has dressed especially for the occasion and this makes me smile. He has been standing waiting for us on the side of the road. I can only imagine what he must be thinking and feeling right now. I am excited to meet him and hop out of the car to greet him. Frank introduces us. He gives me a big, full smile and puts his hand out to greet me. I search his face, looking to see Frankie. Our meeting is much lower key than it was with Frank. We meet on the street and there is little time for conversation, but he is warm toward me. Frank tells him, "This is your sister David. We have a sister from Scotland. Can you believe it?" David hugs me, "It is amazing, Sister. So good to know you. Thank you for coming to Masaka to see me." There are no tears. I'm very composed. I like him. He seems like a nice, caring man. I sense a little apprehension, which is understandable, but he is gracious with me. It must be as surreal for David as it is for me.

David tells us he has found a place for me to buy flowers for his mum. He came to the market earlier, on a scouting mission, to find the *exact* flowers. *Oh, good,* I think to myself.

We start walking toward the market. David says, "So tell me, Sister...do you think I look like my brother?"

"Do you mean Frank or Frankie?"

He laughs, "Ah. Yes, Frankie—our brother, Frankie. Do I look like him?"

I know he wants me to tell him he looks just like him. Perhaps Frank has told him how much they look alike. I sense he wants that reassurance of a connection too.

"You do. Across the eyes you do."

"Oh, that is good. Nice. Very nice. I wish I had met him."

I smile, "Yes. It would have been great."

"But now we have a sister. This is good too."

The market is full of little winding corridors of street vendors crammed into tiny dilapidated structures held together by old corrugated iron, plastic, wood—just about anything people can find. It seems to me they are held together by the will of God and not much else. If there is an infrastructure to the place, I can't see it. The conditions are poor beyond belief. I am glad I am here for flowers and not food. There doesn't seem to be much mindfulness regarding the hygiene of food products strewn on the ground, or other garbage left lying around.

The vendors are even more excited than the children were to see a muzungu. We are the walking wallets. The millionaires. Rony wants a t-shirt made that reads, I AM A MUZUNGU NOT A MILLIONARE. Sadly, it won't make any difference; they believe we are, and nothing we say or do will ever change it. Looking around this market, it's easy to see why they might think so. It's all relative, and in comparison to most people here, I guess we are.

Through every nook and cranny, someone is vying for our attention. It's like a circus—colorful, vibrant and alive. Vendors load their bicycles like an acrobatic juggling act. And, so too do the basket bearers who stack fruits high on their heads. The women wear them like carnival headpieces; swaying this way and that without fear their precious cargo might topple from their crown.

We finally reach a hole-in-a-wall flower shop the size of a cupboard. David proudly presents me with a plastic-wrapped coffin spray that takes up practically the whole shop floor. It is obvious that this vendor has been waiting for us. In fact, all the vendors have been waiting for us. I think my face is saying it all but I try to explain, "It's lovely David. But we only use these for funerals."

David and Frank look perplexed.

Rony is trying not to laugh. He looks at me as if to say, *Let's see you get yourself out of this one, girl.*

I don't want to risk offending anyone. I mean, I have only just met brother number two, and he thinks he has found me the most beautiful flower arrangement for his mother's grave. However, I simply cannot bring myself to purchase this over-the-top funeral tribute. A simple bunch of flowers is all I want. I explain again that in the UK we only use this kind of arrangement on a coffin on the actual day of a funeral.

The boys both nod in unison, "Yes."

It's obviously a cultural thing.

"Did your mum have a favorite color?" I ask.

They both look perplexed again.

"Well, I usually take yellow flowers to Frankie. Can we ask the shop lady for some nice yellow flowers? I want something bright."

"You mean you don't want the funeral flowers, Sister?"

Rony looks like he's about to burst at the seams with laughter. He hands me the camera and starts talking to the shop lady. Before I know it, money changes hands and he is holding a small bunch of beautiful yellow roses. "Job done," he says as he hands them to me.

I hope I haven't offended my new brother, David, and that this misunderstanding hasn't set us off to a bad start. But he seems to be taking my rejection of his floral arrangement okay. At least he keeps saying, "It's okay. It's okay. It's okay. Kale. Kale. Kale"

Another half-hour's drive finds us outside the place Janet once lived as a child with her family. Frank tells me his mother is buried here. It seems that in Uganda, it's not unusual to bury your relatives in the back garden. I'm a little perturbed by this idea. It makes me think about being a child and burying my hamsters at the bottom of the garden. I made small wooden crosses for each of them and Dad always performed touching wee services as we placed them in shoe boxes and put them in the ground. I remember our pet cemetery feeling a tad creepy when I passed by, and this is a big step up from that: actual people at the bottom of the garden.

Janet's house reminds me of a slightly smaller, ransacked version of *Little House on the Prairie*. Her father's small wooden church on the grounds next to it is still standing, just a few feet away from the house. It looks a bit like a primitive car garage with a cross above it, but I'm moved by its simplicity. It's like a beacon of Frankie's lineage, a bygone time in his biological family's life. I romanticize that a few local villagers might have come together with some primitive tools and nails and built this little church by hand. It's a credit to those parishioners that it's still standing here looking magnificently meek.

I have the urge to go in and pray, but the church is padlocked. I'm sad that I'm unable to honor Frankie's grandfather and his family by kneeling down in this humble little church they have built.

Janet's family still owns the land, but there is another family living in the house. They stare at us, even while the boys speak to them in their native language.

Suddenly, the two boys and our driver sling garden hoes over their shoulders. They motion us to follow them through a field of plantain. Apparently, this is the back garden. At least I'm dressed for the occasion with some casual khaki trousers and loose cotton top. I'm learning. But by now I am beginning to panic a little. *Good God, surely not. They're not going to dig her up—are they? Could that be a custom here—to let me have a good look at her?*

It's obvious that no one has been here in a while. The undergrowth we fight our way through seems to be closing in behind us. It is claustrophobic. For the first time in my life, I wish I had a machete. I could chop down the overgrowth of huge banana leaves I'm trying to weave my way through! My skin is getting scratched to bits and bitten by insects. Something runs across my foot. Good God—I hope it's not a rat! I've recently learned from the locals that rats blow on your toes and feet to numb them and then nibble on the skin. At least it didn't feel as big as the rat that crossed my path on the way to my guest room the other night. That one was like a small dog!

Finally, we come to a clearing, and the two boys and the driver start digging. *Oh, God. They really are going to dig her up!* Rony sees the look of horror on my face and asks what their plans are. We are very relieved to find out that they are just clearing the overgrowth from the top of what turns out to be three graves covered in concrete.

The boys begin muttering amongst themselves in their native tongue and jumping feverishly from grave to grave.

"Which one is Janet's?" I ask.

They look at each other. Frank eventually admits he is not sure. It has been eighteen years after all.

Eighteen years since they have visited their deceased mother! There isn't even a headstone. They assure me it is something they have always *meant* to do.

Rony looks at me and mutters, "It's like the three bears. Mummy bear, daddy bear and baby bear. What height was Janet?"

"Five feet, three inches," I tell him. Frank is still weeding around all three of them and David is scratching his head.

"Well, the one Frank thinks it is was for someone about seven feet tall! The middle one is four feet. The last one is probably about six feet."

Despite Rony's calculations, neither of the brothers is sure. Eventually Rony does *eenie meenie minie moe* and chooses a grave. Everyone sighs with relief. Frank and David agree that the one Rony has chosen is probably their mother's. Yes, they have suddenly remembered it is! Hurray!

I still don't know if it's the right one but I kneel down with my yellow roses and am overcome with emotion. I can hardly take it all in. I can't believe that when I arrived in Uganda only a few weeks ago I didn't know anything about Frankie's mother. Now here I am, knelt down at her graveside with his brothers beside me. The emotions are raw—really raw. Losing Frankie and having the painful separation of this mother and child brought to light hits me. I have come on a pilgrimage like no other.

Frank wants to pray. He thanks God for his new sister. He thanks God for leading me here. He thanks God for revealing the truth about his brother in Scotland. He thanks God for how our family has looked after his brother. He thanks Scotland. He thanks Glasgow. He thanks Rony. He thanks the airline that brought us, and the God who brought us here. It's a moving prayer although it is thirty-five minutes too long. I know Rony is praying too—for the word *Amen*.

Once I have composed myself and dried my eyes we are taken to see Frankie's grandfather's grave—just behind Janet's. There's no problem finding him. An ostentatious marble headstone has his name inscribed on it: Rev. Canon Samuel Kaggwa Wevugira. The man lived to be 103! He also died in 1994, the same year as Frankie. I am blown away to discover that he was made a saint. Wow.

David says he has picked a place for his new sister to have lunch in Masaka. I am hoping it's not too expensive since I'm learning the muzungu *always* picks up the check. But mostly I am hoping Frank isn't going to say grace! He does, but mercifully it's unusually short—he must be as hungry as I am. All that graveside weeding has created an appetite.

We sit around a plastic white table on the terrace. The beers and Coca-Colas flow as well as the conversation. The boys relish sharing their life stories with me as well as memories of their mum. It turns out that the two boys haven't seen each other in at least eight years. It feels good being instrumental in bringing them together again.

I want to know how they felt when their mum went to Ireland to study, leaving her young boys behind. I'm surprised when they laugh, even more so when David says they weren't sad at all. "We loved the fact that Mum was in the UK. We got lots of presents sent to us. It was a wonderful time."

Frank pipes up, "And shoes too! Other kids didn't have any shoes, but we did! We got lots of other things sent to us that no one had, even records—especially Elvis Presley. Oh, Mum loved Elvis Presley! Do you remember, David?" Frank starts doing an Elvis Presley impersonation. *"One for the money, two for the show, three to get ready and go cat go."* The boys are taking as much pleasure from their trip down memory lane as I am in listening.

They tell me they lived with Pastor Wevugira and his wife, Miriam, and they were well-taken care of while Janet was studying. I learn Stephen was the first born, then Frank, then David, then Paul. Stephen and Frank were the only brothers who had the same father, but Janet had never married that man.

Janet was certainly not the sweet, innocent young girl I had imagined being swept off her feet and led astray by some charming medical student in Belfast! It seems she was a hot-blooded mamma. My nice little romantic scenario was being blown right out of the water. The question of why Frank was given the same name as Frankie troubles both Frank and David—it's just not done in Uganda. I am beginning to build up theories in my head. I've come this far, so now I want to find out who Frankie's father was but no one seems to know.

I want to ask some questions but I know I have to get to know the boys a bit more before potentially opening up another Pandora's Box. No, right now isn't the time. The conversation is cooling like the sun. Dark clouds are appearing in the stories as the cheerful chat of childhood memories gradually turns to the shocking, turbulent childhood of both David and Frank.

From 1971 to 1979 Uganda suffered harshly under the reign of Idi Amin. Then, after Amin's demise, worse was to come. A raging civil war took place between opposition leader Museveni's National Resistance Army and the government of President Milton Obote from 1981 to 1986. The Bush war, as it became known, was on the doorstep of Luweero, where Janet was teaching at the time. I had written about this violent guerrilla war in Luweero, so at least that gave me a better understanding than most of the complex history and the atrocities that had taken place in this particular area.

Frank tells us how one day the soldiers came and he had to dress up like a girl and hide in one of the bunkers at his mum's school. Museveni had started to conscript child soldiers, so Obote's soldiers saw all male children as a threat. Eventually it got so bad that all children were seen as a threat and the use of landmines became widespread to specifically target young civilians.

Frank shares how one Saturday he went to visit his mum in a neighboring village a few miles walk away. He was tired and decided not to walk back so late at night, staying over with his mum instead. He walked back to his village the next day to discover that every man had been stripped naked and shot dead in his church that morning, and every woman stripped naked and violated. If he had not stayed over with his mother, he too would have been in the church that morning and would have been killed.

The boys go on to tell me of their great escape from the Luweero Triangle—the area later known as the killing fields of Uganda, where millions lost their lives. They tell me how Janet managed to get Red Cross visas via one of her sisters. These cards were like gold and were passes to get them out of Luweero, but to use them they had to get to the Red Cross vehicles miles away from where they were staying.

Frank and David struggle to relate the distressing tale of how they walked for many miles in the heat. They tell me their mum was carrying her youngest son through this danger zone; when she finally got to the Red Cross she collapsed with sheer exhaustion. As the boys speak of this traumatic episode I realize Frankie was perhaps the lucky one after all.

The wounds of war are still deep in Uganda. The history is indelibly printed in the memory of most Ugandans today. The intense competition and fighting for power have left psychological land mines, and if one is not careful, they can be stepped on inadvertently. Tribal bitterness still exists. Much healing still needs to take place.

My new brothers and I come from different worlds. We are connected by a woman who is their mother and her child who was my brother. The connection is real.

The complexities are real. The differences are real. And the emotions are real.

I learn through David and Frank of the deep passion their mother had for teaching and education. Since being here, I've been thinking about building a school in memory of my brother. I tell the boys my dream. My new brothers announce that it has always been their dream to build a school in memory of their mother. It's a beautiful, romantic dream that we share.

Before we head back to Kampala, David wants to show us his home. He tells us it is close by, but I'm learning that could mean it is *miles* away. Thankfully this time it really isn't too far to go.

David is proud of his home, a brick-built, three bedroom bungalow. Unlike similar properties in Scotland, this house is unfinished. There are no glazed windows and no internal doors. The walls aren't plastered and there is no ceiling, just the eves. I'm impressed by David's family home—it's spacious and has much potential. I have already witnessed lots of unfinished construction in Uganda. I don't know how they go about selling houses, but I would love to see some home reports. Of course, if we had Ugandan weather, we in the UK might not finish our homes either.

Much to Frank's surprise, David has a lady friend staying there. It is hard to ascertain the exact position she holds or to whom the children belong, but it seems Frank has some new nieces and nephews and so do I!

David wants to show us his prized possessions. I'm expecting a car or a wide screen TV. Instead we are led into in a side room of his living room where two moth-eaten turkeys flap around wildly. I duck and dive, unprepared to be henpecked by this pair. I look up at the ceiling and there are the remnants of Christmas decorations still in the living room. I wonder if there was another, less lucky, turkey. The stench is overpowering but Rony insists on keeping me there long enough to attempt to pose for his camera with these two big birds. I'm grateful when David suggests tea.

Being Asked to Leave

In my family we used to joke that Frankie could sleep through an earthquake. He frequently slept through his alarm clock and was often late for work. However, because he was so charming, he *mostly* got away with it.

I now know that many black people sleep very deeply—quite differently to white people. I remember reading Michael Caine's biography and his anecdotes about discovering this on one of his trips to Kenya. After trying to wake his personal driver without success and checking his pulse, which he couldn't feel, Michael was convinced the man was dead and called a doctor at two o'clock in the morning. He fully expected him to write a death certificate. However, after checking the driver over, the doctor gave Michael a lecture for waking him up in the middle of the night to attend to a sleeping man. He told him nothing would wake the driver until he was good and ready to wake and suggested he hire himself another driver. I can see our Frankie in this story.

As a young man from Glasgow, Scotland, Frankie enjoyed a fair bit of alcohol. Probably not that much more than any of his peers, but when Frankie drank he seemed to get drunk faster than most – let's just say he could become inebriated.

One Friday night in the early hours of the morning, when everyone else was sleeping, Frankie came home drunk and with a beery-hunger. His ritual was to put toast under the grill—not a toaster which would pop the toast up when it was ready, but a grill under the cooker. Frankie then went into the living room and subsequently fell sound asleep while the toast burned away to a crisp under the grill.

I hadn't long gone to bed myself when I smelled the smoke, ran down stairs and possibly saved us all from a house fire. I somehow managed to get Frankie up to his bed before Mum or Dad was woken by the smell of smoke. Of course, the next morning Mum did notice someone had buttered the video recorder in the living room—like I say, inebriated.

The next time, I wasn't there to cover for him. It was Mum who, fortunately, woke up and smelled the burning toast. The only way she could get Frankie to wake up that night was to throw a few glasses of cold water over him. He was oblivious to the potential threat of disaster she had just averted. The combination of being a deep sleeper and too much alcohol was deadly, and my parents knew it.

Frankie didn't have good judgment when it came to people—seen through his eyes, everyone was nice. It was like a filter was missing when it came to judging a person's character. Don't get me wrong, he did have some wonderful friends, many of whom I'm still in touch with to this day. But he was a total sucker for people with sob stories—especially women. Sometimes he'd bring them back to the house. I remember one girl in particular who got up during the night and robbed us blind. She was a very clever little thief—we didn't discover the theft until Mum and I were at the checkout in the supermarket and realized that all Mum's credit cards and cash were gone out of her handbag. You can imagine Mum's embarrassment.

At first, Mum thought Frankie had stolen her cash and cards. It's sad but true that he had, on occasion, stolen money from her purse. Not much, just a few pounds or a fiver here and there. It was the principle that Mum couldn't get her head around. It went back to the early days of him stealing food; why steal food when there is enough? Why steal money? He only had to ask her if he was short. And, just like the food as an infant, he'd tell her he hadn't taken the money. Then he'd admit it; then he'd promise he was going to give it all back to her—with interest!

Frankie was always full of good intentions, *great* intentions even, and all his intentions were genuine. There was not a mean or bad bone in Frankie's body; that was what made it so hard to be angry with him. But when it came to Mum, he eventually managed to make her angry. He didn't once steal money from Dad's wallet or mine. I hate writing this because I feel as if I am betraying Frankie by doing so; it is so difficult to be open about all the truths of our past. But I know there is no point in writing about the difficulties that can arise with *some* adoptions if I gloss over the specific issues we faced as a family.

Think about this from a mother's perspective. If an adoptive mother offers a child her home, her love and everything she has and that child hurts her by lying, stealing, or almost setting the house on fire, then no matter how much she can try to understand the psychological wounds of that little soul, it still hurts—really hurts! Mum was hurting.

Some might argue that Frankie's case was unique; it was and is, just like all children and all adoptions are unique. However, having read *The Primal Wound* by Nancy Newton Verrier, I have learned that it is not uncommon for the adoptive child to steal from the one person whose affection and attention the child craves the most—usually the mother.

A psychologist might call it testing behavior. A self-fulfilling prophecy. In the end Mum and Dad—very reluctantly—had to ask Frankie to leave the family home. Frankie had perpetuated his own myth that he wasn't worthy of a mother's love and that one day Mum would abandon him just like his biological mother had done.

Although Frankie was in his early twenties by this stage, the pain resonated in each one of our family members. We subconsciously knew the wounds were different from that of a biological child being asked to leave the family home. But the truth was that as much as they loved him, he was, at times, a danger to himself and the family.

Frankie laughing at Dad's dry sense of humor

I think Dad, in particular, had enormous difficulty asking Frankie to move out. Dad would have adopted more children. Being honest, I expect it was partly to help him unravel his own emotions, because he genuinely wanted to give children a secure, lovely environment—something he himself had lacked. It was evident, even within my friendship groups, that he wanted children to feel safe and secure. Many of my friends saw my dad as their second father and our home was always open to waifs and strays. Many of my generation would say to this day that my dad had a profound impact on their lives. But no matter how much good Dad did with other children, I know he also felt he had failed Frankie in some way. Although of course, he hadn't. I don't believe he could have done any more to help him. Frankie and Dad adored each other—there was always laughter and playful affection between them. Perhaps their ease with each other enlarged the tensions between Mum and Frankie, but as a father and husband, he sincerely tried to address the conflict between Frankie and Mum.

The really sad irony is that the house fire in which Frankie died was due to a power failure and a total accident. Perhaps if Frankie hadn't been such a deep sleeper, he might have woken up before it was too late. But sadly this wasn't to be.

CHAPTER SIX
Grandma Miriam

Uganda, 2012

Frankie's grandma lives in a parish called Vvumba, in the district of Luweero approximately forty kilometers from Kampala and just twenty kilometers from Gayaza High School. Phibi has arranged for us to visit; she believes so sincerely that God has brought me to Uganda for a reason and that my meeting her at Gayaza was divine providence. It's hard to argue with the amazing synchronicity.

Even though Grandma Miriam is not Frankie's maternal grandmother, to me it is the same as if she is. I am still not sure of the wisdom of telling Janet's secret to the older generation, but Phibi reassures me that her aunt Miriam will be sympathetic to the circumstances and that I have nothing to fear.

As is customary, Frank, who hasn't actually seen his grandmother in over thirteen years, wants to buy her some gifts. I expect Frank might be asking our driver to stop the car to buy some flowers or the equivalent of a box of Ferrero Rocher, but once again Uganda and its customs surprise me.

First, we stop at some roadside vendors to find the sweetest pineapples. After much scrutiny of literally hundreds of pineapples strewn on the ground, Phibi and Frank pick out about a dozen and load them into the back of the car. Further along the road we stop for the staple of the Ugandan diet, matoke—huge branches of these green banana-like plantains are ubiquitous in Uganda and they take up most of the trunk of the car. Matoke might look like bananas but don't be fooled; when in an unripe state, which is the state in which they are most commonly used, it needs to be cooked—and well cooked. Its flesh is hard due to the heavy starch content and so it is steamed or roasted before consumption. Once cooked, the flesh turns to orange and its texture is like turnip but that's where the similarity ends. It's totally tasteless. Thankfully, we also pick up some of the yellow bananas that are more familiar to my palate.

Everywhere you look in Uganda there is food. Small kiosks and stalls line every road. Color and texture fight for attention like the vendors themselves, both in the towns and countryside. No one in Uganda should ever go hungry—in theory at least. The land is so fertile; I am sure if I planted myself in it I would grow. It has the perfect climate for most crops. However, the distribution of the harvest from the land leaves a lot to be desired. One in three children has no food to eat during the day and more than half the population is eating way less than they need. It's surprising in a country that claims to produce more food than it can consume. Yet, poverty still limits access to good nutritious food.

Our next stop is a small grocery shop where Frank buys bread, rice, and soap for his grandmother. I ask what I should buy as a gift and am told to buy bottled water. I would have preferred something more frivolous like a beautiful scarf, a china teapot, perfume, or scented candles. Or how about a nice piece of jewelry? But I oblige and fill what is left of the trunk with my practical gift.

By the time we finish, the car looks like a small kiosk. Pyramids of pineapples, mounds of matoke, bunches of bananas—and not a chocolate or flower in sight.

We don't have to go too far along a tree-lined red murram dust road in the rural village before we come to Grandma Miriam's home. We stop at her small stone house, which has a huge ant hill sitting off to one side. An old dog who had been lounging on the rickety porch gets up from its spot to greet us with as much enthusiasm as it can muster in the heat.

A visit with Grandma Miriam

Sadly, we are not greeted at the door by Miriam as I had imagined. On entry to her humble home, I discover Grandma Miriam is paralyzed from the waist down and has been for at least eight years. As is her sister, who sits opposite, bookending her in the living room. I'm told there in no connection to their disabilities. Phibi tells me it's a combination of things that has caused both her aunts to be paralyzed from the waist down. Miriam, I'm told was a fatty big lady at one point and fell down and got a bad fracture, then a foot ulcer. I'm glad being called a fatty big lady isn't necessarily an insult in Uganda.

But now these two frail old ladies, legs outstretched and covered in blankets, sit like the epitome of grace in later life. Arms with skin like parchment covering thin bones reach out as far as they can to greet us all with warm hugs. Their broad, pink-lipped, toothless smiles are absolutely endearing as is their obvious excitement at this meeting.

They are both wearing their busuuti and I am deeply touched.

I can see that Miriam has little in the way of possessions, but I know instinctively that what she lacks materially, she makes up for in richness of experience. Her body is etched with the ravages of time. She reminds me of an old gnarled tree trunk that has stood for centuries. If you could see inside, you could count the rings. But her face is mild, gentle with soft saggy wrinkles.

Her sister, however, is like a Tutankhamun's mummy. She is obviously well into her nineties—if not her hundreds—and looks as though she has been unwrapped from her bandages especially for our visit.

I sit down beside Miriam, who immediately holds my hands. Phibi starts to tell her the story of Frankie in her native tongue. Frank sits to my other side and holds my hand. He joins in excitely to tell his grandmother all about his brother in Scotland. I'm overwhelmed. Here I am sitting enveloped by Frankie's relatives in Uganda. I *know* Frankie is here with us! Miriam keeps her eyes firmly on mine and starts stroking my hands. Tears well up in her eyes as Phibi and Frank relate the tale. Miriam grasps my hands even tighter. Phibi tells me that Frank is explaining to her how Frankie and I were like twins, and how hard his death was on me. Miriam looks at me with such sympathy and then gives me the biggest hug, holding on to me as tight as she can.

This woman is not sitting in judgment of Janet or me. I sense she aches inside for the pain Janet must have felt giving up her child.

Phibi tells me Miriam is saying she is sad that Janet had to carry her secret on her own. She tells them she wishes she had known and could have helped Janet in some way. I am told she is saying she is grateful to me for coming and I am now her granddaughter. She says I have made an old lady very happy today. She thanks God for bringing me to her and telling her the truth. She thanks me for being a good sister to Janet's son.

Miriam does not speak any English, but she doesn't have to for me to know what she is thinking and feeling. She looks at me with such an endearing smile that I can trust she really is grateful for my pilgrimage and is somehow better off for this knowledge. I had feared the truth might destroy this mother's image of Janet, but now I feel I have actually enhanced it in the eyes of this old soul.

Miriam is eager to see the photo album I have brought. She takes her time, taking in every detail. She quickly remarks how much Frank looks like Frankie. Frank's face lights up when anyone says this. After looking at all the photographs, she reaches for the Bible sitting next to her. She picks it up and unzips it like it holds some precious treasure—and it turns out that it does. From its worn pages she produces a picture of Frankie's grandfather in his Army Chaplains uniform. Wow, I can't believe I am finally seeing a photograph of Pastor Wevugira. He looks so refined. She then shows me her wedding picture. It's an immense thrill to see these photographs. I think she feels a similar thrill at showing them to me. Her eyes are alive and sparkling as she remembers herself on her wedding day; she smiles and giggles like a teenager.

Grandma Miriam on her wedding day to
Frankie's grandfather

The old black and white photographs Miriam shows me make Frankie's family look like landed gentry. Some of the family look like caricatures of white people!

But I know from my research that many did in those days. Still, to see Frankie's lineage looking like this is both comical and endearing. They were a well-educated group by the looks of them, and proud landowners. Pastor Wevugira was obviously highly revered in the community.

As I look at photographs of Miriam, barely twenty years old, I think how difficult it must have been for her to take on four girls and five boys who had lost their biological mamma as well as a much older man of the clergy. But I can see in the photographs that, even in her youth, Miriam was made of the right stuff—tough, yet tender.

Miriam's young helpers have been busy preparing a feast for us in the back garden. Most kitchens in Uganda are outside. It is amazing what a variety of food can be made on small wooden charcoal stoves in the ground and how much can be fitted onto a small wooden table!

Everything we brought with us has been magically transformed into a banquet fit for a king. The only thing we didn't bring with us was the chicken. However, I have already decided it would be safer to eat like a vegetarian while in Uganda, so I gracefully decline the grilled chicken—again, and again and again.

After my vegetarian feast, I am shown the back garden and introduced to—no, not a grave—but two small chickens running around. Phibi tells me they just lost a sibling.

"Oh, dear," I say. "That is such a shame."

Phibi tilts her head to the side and clasps her hands in front of her stomach. "Yes, it is my dear. He was killed in *your* honor."

I am horrified at my obvious faux pas and go back to the table to repent and eat the chicken, only to find that the Tutankhamun mummy has scoffed the lot! I can't believe this frail old woman's appetite—it is insatiable.

To the right-hand side of Miriam are a pile of raffia mats made out of palm leaves. As we are getting ready to leave, she pulls one from the pile and gifts it to me. I am moved by her kindness.

Miriam doesn't want me to leave, I can tell. She keeps hold of my hand and affectionately strokes it. She asks to pray with me and leads us all in an emotional prayer of thanksgiving to God for the miracle of today and for the family in Scotland who loved and cared for Frankie until he was reunited with Janet in heaven. After saying *Amen*, she starts softly singing an old spiritual song that I know well from my childhood, "Kumbaya, my Lord". Everyone in the room joins in.

The Wounded Healer

Dad often laughed about his "shameful" upbringing. In today's society his illegitimacy wouldn't even raise an eyebrow. But it is amazing how shame functions in families and how twisted the road to good intentions can become.

He always knew something wasn't right, that he felt different in some way. Dad couldn't explain it, but he knew that there was a secret surrounding him. Children are much more intuitive than we give them credit for and from an early age he had learned to read between the lines. Dad often said to me the most shameful secrets are exposed by their silence. He taught me to listen carefully to what people *didn't* say. It was a good lesson.

After the de-closeting of Dad's illegitimacy, he claimed that coming partly from unknown stock gave him a feeling of all things being possible. It was as if it gave him permission to stand apart from the crowd, to develop a different interior from the rest of the family. Dad's illegitimacy somehow released him from his family shackles. However, the deep wound of being rejected by a mother he knew and a father he didn't, and the shame surrounding his birth, left a painful hole in his heart.

Our beautiful dad

Dad was also a premature baby and therefore taken directly from his biological mother and put in an incubator. It's not surprising he arrived early considering that there had been two failed home abortion attempts. Dad was a born fighter. There have been studies done to suggest that children who are incubated directly from birth have some of the same abandonment issues as those of adopted children. I have often wondered that if his mother had been allowed to hold him after his birth, if her maternal instinct might have kicked in and the pair of them would have had a chance to bond.

You'd be hard pushed to know that Dad was minister of the Church of Scotland. He was very liberal, totally down to earth and had a great sense of humor and drama. We didn't pray at the dinner table, and he didn't deliver biblical text at home. I think he had a bit of an aversion to the indoctrination of small children. Of course, we were baptized and brought up with what I would say were Christian morals, but Dad believed in each person's right to choose their own spiritual path—or none at all. We did attend Sunday School but were never forced to go. Neither were we forced to read the Bible or quote biblical text.

Dad didn't expect Mum to attend church either. After all, she had married a handsome, rugged bulldozer driver whose aspirations were more Hollywood than heavenly. Mum and Dad loved to tell the story of his road-to-Damascus experience. People were always curious about his dramatic conversion, so it became a bit of a party piece known as *the morning after the night before*. This is how I remember Mum relating it to me when I was in my teens.

"The day your father told me he'd found God, I thought he was still drunk from the night before or had progressed to drugs. I swear you could have knocked me over. I thought he was having a laugh and enjoying winding me up. He had been out all night on a bender and there he was, standing in front of me still reeking of booze, dripping wet, telling me he'd gone into a church and spoken to God, and he was going to become a minister. He'd never been in a church in his life!" Mum laughed. "I knew your father was bonkers when I married him, but this was his craziest stunt yet."

"What did you do, Mum?"

"I told him to go to bed and sleep it off. Didn't I, William?" She nudged Dad, who was pretending not to listen.

Dad faked a yawn. "Ah, but I didn't sleep it off. And I still haven't, all these years later."

"I'll never understand what happened to your father that day, but when he woke up he was still high. You'd have thought he'd won the football pools—I wish he had because we were destitute. But your dad kept saying he'd found something better than gold—he had found God. Honestly, I was ready to pack my bags and leave him and God to it!"

"Och Och, your mum was just concerned that there'd be no more sex! She somehow equated me finding God with becoming celibate. I kept telling her it's only Catholic priests that have to give up sex, not Church of Scotland ministers."

"I did not!" She slapped him playfully on the shoulder, pretending to be embarrassed. "I just wasn't so sure I'd fancy you in that big black cassock. I happened to like your long curls hanging down over your face and those tight trousers and work boots. Look at you now— all suited up."

Mum wasn't your typical minister's wife. Frankly, she would have looked more at home gracing a catwalk rather than a church aisle. She kept hoping to find the kind of faith Dad had found, but her faith was always rooted in him rather than in God. Still, Mum took her role as a minister's wife seriously. As busy as she was raising three children and working as a full-time nurse, she still found time to join the choir, the Monday Night club, the Woman's Guild and to attend every coffee morning she could. She baked, knitted, sang, *and* she drank—well, she had the odd tipple or two.

After the congregation's initial shock at her long hippy skirts, Afghan coats, and beads, they loved her. She was the perfect hostess, loving nothing more than a party—as did Dad. The manse was always full of people. Mum loved to sing, her favorite being Barbara Streisand. Dad surprised her one day by going out and buying an amplifier, two big Marshall speakers and a microphone. No one had this kind of gear in their homes in those days, unless they were a pop star or in a band. It was amazing, and unsurprisingly the parties became even more popular. The manse was like the local karaoke club before that trend came to Glasgow. The cultural and social diversity was incredible, with conversation and drinks flowing till the early hours.

The comedy and tragedy of people's lives were what made the manse such a tremendous place to grow up. Mum and Dad rolled with the punches and there was always a spare bed for someone in dire straits. I learned from a young age that life is not easy and people can find themselves in unbelievably bad situations.

Divorce, financial ruin, loss of a child, scandal, drugs, alcohol, suicide, rape – you name it, Dad dealt with it. Even if some of the details were a little shady for children's ears, I learned to read between the lines.

Dad was not afraid to fight for justice and to confront the law. He used his agile mind to help the underdogs of his congregation and his friends. Our life was peppered with many people, not just 'the Christians' as Dad would sometimes jokingly refer to his flock, but judges, lawyers, theologians, politicians, football players, drug addicts, alcoholics, gangsters, prisoners, the tortured, the mentally ill and the victims of rape. Dad knew them both confidentially as a minister and as a friend. He helped them out when they needed him. People trusted him; although Dad had found God, he was still a man of the people and equally as at home in the pub or in the pulpit.

Dad did his best to protect his family from the harsher realities, but at the same time he didn't shelter us from the awareness that life could throw some pretty big storms into the lives of even the nicest of people. From a young age, I learned that no one was immune to pain, that it was part of life. This was a valuable lesson.

I wish there was *one* word to describe my father, but he was many things to many people. At his funeral, Dad's friend and fellow minister described him as "the Wounded Healer." Whatever deep wounds were left in Dad from the painful rejection by his biological mother and father, he was somehow able to overcome them and in so doing help others navigate their own pain and darkness.

I adored my father. But even as a child, I knew he was wounded. He appeared to the world as very together, charming, funny, intelligent, and compassionate—and he really was all of those things. But he was also lonely, depressed, misunderstood and insecure. I know this because my dad wrote all the time, not just sermons but lyrics, poems, and journals. He had even started a libretto for a musical and after his death, as with Frankie's adoption papers, I inherited it all. Sometimes I wish I hadn't been privy to them, but what I read was a window into his soul.

While writing this book and going through the paperwork I inherited, I came across some letters my dad wrote to the General Register Office for Scotland in 1993. The date ties in with Frankie's request to know more about his biological family. I had previously overlooked these letters as they weren't in Frankie's adoption file.

It looks like Dad had been trying to obtain Certificates of Birth for them both. Unfortunately, as they were both adopted he was only able to receive an extract of their original birth entries rather than the more conventional full Certificate of Birth which includes the time of birth, residence, and the name of both parents. He was eventually successful at getting a time of birth sent to him. However, it was obvious from the letters back and forth that Dad wanted to know if his father's name was on the original documents. It would seem that frightening curiosity had eventually got the better of him too.

It's a Wise Man who Knows His own Father

Uganda, 2012

It's my last day in Uganda. Frank tells me he wants to take me to his church and then to visit his dad. I assume that means after church we are going to another grave. Frank has hardly mentioned his father in the three weeks we've been here, but he obviously wants me to go. So, out of respect I tell him that would be nice.

I'm surprised Frank is not with the Ugandan Church he was indoctrinated into by his grandfather. He tells me he left the Church of Uganda to join the Pentecostal Assemblies of God because the Church of Uganda let him down when his friend died of AIDS.

Frank is almost electric when he talks about the Watoto church. He's excited to take me there. I have seen the gaudy ten-foot-high adverts for the church all over Kampala: they are hard to miss. The over-sell of this church doesn't impress me, but I am prepared to give Frank's church the benefit of the doubt for his sake.

As we drive toward the church the traffic is piling up by the minute. Frank points enthusiastically to a huge white marquee in the distance. "There it is. That is the church."

Wow. It's like a venue for a rock concert. Our car and bags are searched for bombs and guns then finally we are shown where to park the car—miles away. There must be over two thousand people here.

The tented venue is rigged with enough lighting and sound gear for a Rolling Stones concert.

The band starts up and they are good. I mean, really good. I know why everyone is here—for this incredible gospel music. They play a full forty-five minute set. I get right into the music. I love it, all the people singing and dancing and really whipping themselves into a frenzy. But this is just the warm-up act before the main act— the pastor.

The lights change on cue and with them so does the mood. The *messiah* has appeared! Is that dry ice I see? Hey, hold on, he's white. I'm disappointed. I kind of hoped there would be a black preacher. I was looking for someone like the James Brown character from the Blues Brothers film. But this white man welcomes us all with his wide-open, white arms. Hold on a minute—that's a Canadian accent. I have lived in Canada for eighteen years and never heard of him, yet he is a superstar over here.

It's a two-hour marathon of hellfire and brimstone over the subject of tithing. Basically, we are being told we must give ten percent of everything we have and everything we earn—otherwise, God will punish us. But if we give to the church, God will reward us.

Neon quotes from the Old and New Testaments flash on and off on the screens to reinforce the word of God. If the preacher says tithing once, he says it two hundred times. He tells us how he lives modestly and drives a modest car. He subjects the congregation to a massive guilt trip just before the collections baskets are handed round.

Members of the congregation look and sound like they've devoured more LSD than fans at a '60s rock concert. Some of them even start speaking in tongues—even Frank does. I'm sure more people go down to the stage to be touched by this preacher than Elvis ever received. Personally, I am more drawn to his sweaty, brow-mopping sidekick choir leader. I can't keep my eyes off him: think James Brown meets Mick Jagger.

It's movie time. The big, wide screen in front of us shows us some well-constructed documentaries about the wonderful work Watoto Church is doing for the orphans in Uganda—in particular, the AIDS victims. I'm moved by the films they show. They are well produced but I do wonder if there could be a bit of child exploitation going on here. This church may well be assisting these kids—they are showing us evidence that seems to prove they are doing a great job—but where does one draw the line between help and exploitation?

It takes us at least thirty minutes to get out of the Watoto car park and away from the guard who wants to charge Rony for smoking a cigarette. Fortunately, the offer of one from his pack is enough to ensure he puts his gun down.

Frank wants to know what I think about his church. I don't want to insult him. I tell him it was very different from our churches back home and it was like going to a rock concert. I tell him the churches back home are pretty much empty these days. He can't believe it. Everyone in Uganda goes to church. I laugh and tell him maybe the churches back home should be producing shows like today's to entice people back into the fold. I tell him, rightly or wrongly, a preacher who talks about tithing in our country probably wouldn't have a congregation. He is shocked.

We negotiate the Kampala traffic for about an hour, talking about the differences between churches back home in Scotland and in Uganda. When I tell him old church buildings in the UK are being turned into nightclubs and bars he simply can't believe it. In Uganda, new churches are being built every day.

Frank's dad

All this talk helps the journey go quickly. We soon arrive in a small suburb, where Frank asks the driver to stop outside what looks like another small hole-in-the-wall shop. I think he's just stopped to pick up something—perhaps some flowers for his father's grave? Frank motions us to get out the car. *Oh, great. Do I have to buy the flowers?* We follow Frank into a dimly lit, narrow room. Sitting in the corner is a petite, frail old man dressed in collar and tie, wearing a Chicago Bulls basketball cap and large rimmed glasses. He is reading a newspaper and listening to a sports channel on the radio.

"Dad, I have brought some friends from Scotland to meet you."

Oh, my God! Frank's father is still alive. The old man looks up from his paper. The baseball cap and spectacles take up practically his entire face so I can hardly see his features. I guess that once upon a time the spectacles fitted his face nicely. He puts the paper down and shakes hands with us. He offers us a seat. There is a row of wooden chairs lined up against the wall, and we each pick one to sit on. I'm thinking this must be some kind of small office dwelling— although there is nothing obvious to suggest *what* exactly it is.

Frank and his dad exchange a conversation in their native tongue. I think Frank is telling them about Frankie, but I can't be sure until Frank asks me for the photographs of Frankie. Frank sits beside his father and shows them to him. His father shows little to no reaction as Frank narrates the story.

His father finally starts to communicate in English.

"I told you to try and find the boy when you first heard about him—did I not?"

Mmm, I'm thinking, *his father's rather defensive.* Frank looks somewhat cowardly in front of this tiny man.

His father looks at the photograph of Frankie in the kilt and tells us he wore one of those at school and how much he loved it. I surmise that he was well educated in a private school.

He looks up at Frank. "Did you tell them about Janet?" He speaks as if we are not in the room.

Frank says, "A little."

What did he *not* tell me?

The old man continues to look through the photograph album, pushing the large glasses back onto his nose now and then.

Everyone else we have met has been curious about the circumstances surrounding Frankie. There have always been lots of questions from people and comments on how much he looks like Frank, but this man isn't saying anything or asking any questions. He just sits with his arms folded in front of his chest, letting Frank go through the pictures one by one.

Finally, Frank says, "Don't you think he looks like me, Dad? Here especially. Look."

He nods. "Yes, yes I can see some resemblance."

Frank goes on, "He even has the same name as me."

His father doesn't remark that it is strange he has the same name, as others do. There is an awkward silence. Eventually, his father asks, "Where is this boy now?"

Frank tells him he died in a fire. His father folds his arms even tighter across his chest and does a little seat shuffle. He says nothing. Now, this I find even stranger. Most people say something when they hear he died. At the very least they say they are sorry to hear that. But he doesn't say anything.

I remember Frank said his father had been to the UK and my gut instinct kicks in. Good God, could he have been in the UK when Janet was there? Could this be Frankie's father sitting here, right in front of me? It suddenly adds up. The name Frank. Frank was born before Frankie; they could have had the same father. Could Janet have been leaving a trace back to the father—the name means "a boy who knows his father." Frank has been upset about the fact that they both have the same name and keeps asking why his mother would do such a thing, but this could have been a clue she was trying to leave for Frankie's future. Has Frank suspected this all along?

I turn to his father, "Frank told me you've been to the UK."

"Yes, yes. I liked the UK. It was good."

"Did you see Janet when you were in the UK?"

He does his little seat shuffle again. "Oh, yes. I went to visit with her a few times. I was studying to be a medical administrator and traveled a fair bit in the UK—different hospitals. I was lucky—I got to go all over the UK."

Bloody hell, I'm thinking. *So this is the medical student—this guy really is the father! He's the one who must have arranged for Janet to go to Scotland in secret and have her baby. He could have easily set it up.* I want to hit him! I want to yell at him: *You self-righteous son of a bitch! Tell us the bloody truth.* But he sits there looking complacent and doesn't even ask anything about Frankie. I remember what my father told me, "It's what people don't say, Michaela. Listen to what they don't say. The truth is in the silence."

Frank's father tells me again how he was very good friends with Janet. *Oh, I'll bet you were.* I'm thinking to myself. *I'd say you were a bit more than friends. You had two, possibly three children together. One of them, I'm guessing, was my brother. Who you left in Scotland, in a children's home! If it hadn't been for my parents then God only knows where he could have ended up.*

Oh, I am seething inside, but for Frank's sake I'm trying hard to "keep the heid" as we say in Glasgow.

I want to turn this man upside down and shake the truth out of him. At the very least I want to pull off his baseball cap and large glasses and check out his face. I want to see if I can spot a proper resemblance to Frankie.

I have to fold my hands between my legs to stop myself from whipping his cap off. Instead I go on with my interrogation. "How often did you manage to see Janet in the UK?"

"Oh, not much. Holidays mainly. Christmas time and New Year. We got a break around then, and I went to see her in Belfast."

Bingo! It doesn't take a genius to figure all this out. He wasn't going there for a cup of tea and Christmas cake—he was going there for his nookie! How many months between January and September? Nine. The length of a pregnancy.

They say the truth will always come out in the end. Everyone in the room knows, but no one is saying anything. Why doesn't Frank just ask the question I know he wants to ask? But he remains quiet—unusually so.

"What was Janet like?" I ask, hoping to see his eyes light up from behind those big glasses. I'm still searching for a shred of romance to my brother's conception in Belfast.

"Oh, Janet was good fun." He shuffles again smiling this time. "She was always laughing, always smiling. She was good fun."

Good fun—I'll say. I tell him Frankie was like that too. Always laughing and smiling. I tell him it sounds like Frankie took after his mother.

He looks at me for the first time. "It's a good trait to have. Being able to laugh is a gift. You know Janet and I were good friends. Good friends till the day she died."

Oh, how I want him to tell me if he knows he is the father. I look over at Frank. We both know we are thinking the same thing. Did he talk Janet into the adoption? Did he arrange for her to go to Scotland? We both know this man has all those answers, but he's still holding onto the family secret as tightly as his arms are folded across his chest.

The old man passes Frank the photograph album and reaches for his newspaper, which we take as a sign that we are to leave. He moves out of his chair with difficulty. This might be the first and last time I ever see him. I am gracious and tell him how wonderful it was to meet him. I give him a hug. He says, "Thank you for coming to visit me. It was good to meet you. It's good to know Frank has a sister."

When we are all safely outside, I ask Frank, "Are you thinking what I am thinking?"

"Yes. I think so."

"Then why could you not have asked him outright if he was Frankie's father?"

Frank's head is down. He says he wanted to, but it's just not done in Uganda. He tells me he could never ask his father a question like that.

All the questions I wanted to ask the old man I now heap on top of Frank, but he has none of the answers. Finally, he is saved from my onslaught by his phone ringing. It's his father. Frank speaks to him in Luganda while I hang on to every foreign word, hoping that it's confession time. Frank hangs up.

"What did he say? Did he admit he was the father?"

"No. He just wanted to know what you muzungus wanted."

Frankie's father might have thought that when he left little Francis behind in Scotland he would never see or hear anything about him again. But now, as an old man, the past is coming back to haunt him. If he really is the father then he just got to see pictures of his son and hear about his life in Scotland.

It's strange though. My reaction to meeting Frankie's father is so different from what I would have expected. I'm not moved; I'm angry. I am not sure where the anger has come from, or why I want to lash out at him. I really want to ask him how he felt about abandoning his son in a country full of white people in the '60s. I want to ask him if he knows how much pain a child feels when taken from his mother at birth and how much pain a mother feels. I want to witness some remorse from this man. I want to tell him my brother was too good for him and I'm glad he didn't grow up with him. I want to tell him what he missed out by not knowing my brother.

The Broken Plate

Uganda, 2012

After our visit with Frank's dad, Frank arranges for Rony and me to have dinner at his home. The house belongs to his dad, and Frank shares it with his half-sister, Violet, and her daughter.

It's a lovely home—above the standard of most I've seen so far. In fact, I am well impressed; they even have a VIP loo rather than the usual hole in the ground.

We sit together on the porch while the ladies of the house prepare the food. Frank cannot believe that Rony is the one who cooks back home and is more domesticated than me. Very few men cook in the family home in Uganda. Many believe a man cooking at home is degrading. Frank thinks he has to teach his new sister a thing or two about Ugandan customs or I will not be accepted in his country. However, today is a special day. As it is the first time I have visited Frank's home, I am allowed to relax with the men on the porch and have a Coca-Cola.

My curious mind is working overtime about Frank's half-sister, Violet. Frank has already told me she is older than him. So there has to have been another woman in

Frank's father's life before Janet. If I had a glass of wine in my hand rather than a Coca-Cola, I would probably have asked the question by now and without much delicacy. Eventually I ask Frank about Violet's mother with as much subtlety as I can muster.

Frank tells me Violet's mother got married to his father when they were both young. After Violet was born it was discovered that his wife had mental health problems and she was put into a residential hospital for the mentally ill. Frank then tells me shortly after her incarceration his father started a relationship with Janet, who was twenty years, his junior.

He explains they had wanted to get married, but because his first wife was still living, and the delicate circumstance surrounding her health, he was not allowed to marry Janet. However, everyone in the community accepted their relationship. "After all," he says, "men have needs and his wife was in an institution."

Stephen was the first born from this new relationship. Then Frank. Then—well—my guess is Frankie.

Wow. The jigsaw puzzle is really starting to come together.

It's a beautiful day. The view from the porch looking out over the walled garden is especially lovely. No flowers are planted in the garden, but it has tremendous potential for those with green fingers. Frank wants to show us his farm. I'm relieved when he tells me it is outside, around the back of this house, rather than in a room.

A small goat hut and a makeshift chicken coop make up Frank's farm. He asks me how many goats and chickens I have in my home, and is utterly shocked when I tell him I don't keep any—either in my house or my garden! He'd assumed we would have lots of goats and chickens running around in Scotland. I try to explain what my flat is like in Glasgow, but he has a difficult time believing that we don't keep animals and I don't own masses of land.

We go back to sitting on the porch, looking through lots of old family photograph albums. I can't believe I am learning so much about Frankie's biological family. I'm taken aback by just how alike Stephen, Frank and David were to Frankie in their youth.

Family albums must have been difficult for my adopted brother. They will have emphasized the void in his life, the sense of not knowing where he came from when other families had vast albums of their roots. Frankie had to create his own idea of his lineage, like other adopted children. I wonder if he made up old photographs in his head.

Once again, I have to pinch myself: here I am looking straight into Frankie's biological family's history, in his family home in Uganda. But maybe he's here in his own way, right beside me, looking over my shoulder. It certainly feels that way.

Violet prepares an exquisite meal. Frank knows my love of fish and is excited to show me the Nile perch he has bought especially for me. Violet and her daughter set out a feast on the living room table for us to help ourselves. The steamed fish is wrapped in banana leaves and smells delicious. The avocados and spinach fight for my attention, as do the steamed matoke, rice and potatoes. I heap what I think is loads onto my plate but it's still not enough to satisfy Frank—he thinks his new sister is far too skinny and needs to eat more.

I take my plate over to the couch and sit down. I place it on my lap and wait for Frank to say grace. Just after he has finished, the plate on my lap breaks cleanly in two with an audible snap! Everyone freezes as if a gun has just fired. They stare at the intact food arrangement still sitting on my lap, with the plate underneath now in two pieces. I sense embarrassment and anxiety coming from Frank and Violet. They start fussing in case I am hurt. They tell me that a plate has never *ever* broken in their house before. I can sense they are superstitious— so am I.

I think quickly and tell them that in Greece this is a sign of happiness, that it is the custom for Greeks to break plates at weddings and special occasions of celebration.

"Really!" they chorus. They have never heard of this custom.

I assure them this is a good sign—that I love Greece and even wrote an album about Greek mythology.

"Yes, yes, Sister, this must be good. Good, we are happy, this is a good sign."

How can I tell them my inner thoughts about the symbolism of the broken plate and adoption? Is Frankie trying to tell me something from the other side or what!

Okay, maybe it's a total fluke, a strange coincidence that my plate snapped in two. I have no idea, but no one else's plate broke, and I have never had anything like that happen to me before. Nor have they. They assure me they are good plates, the very best. I am sure they are.

I feel certain Frankie is telling me something. He's reminding me of how he felt all his life. Frankie had experienced a break in the continuity of bonding. Our family was like a glue that bonded him to us, but the trust in his environment has been compromised from birth. His plate had been broken, and although the replacement piece was good and the glue strong, he must have felt he only ever had a tenuous hold. The plate could break again at any time. Now, his family and I have been brought together. These fragile pieces of history are being glued back together after years of separation, of being lost to each other and now, I myself am a piece from a broken plate.

If I was Japanese I would have the crack of the plate on my lap glued together again with a precious metal of gold or silver. A technique called Kintsugi or "Golden Joinery" would give a new lease of life to the broken plate and enhance its "scar" so it could be admired. The repaired plate would become unique because of the randomness of where it was cracked. It would become a work of art with its own beauty and story. I love the symbolism that once the crack is repaired it becomes of more value. It is the essence of resilience. To find beauty in broken things and for our wounds in life to make us more unique and valuable.

I think about asking to keep the plate but I doubt my new Ugandan family will understand my desire to keep a broken object and might think me rather odd. I am sure the broken plate will be confined to the bin.

CHAPTER SEVEN
STARCHILD—the charity

After we return from Uganda, Rony and I put together a collection of some of our photographs and videos. The presentation of my "pilgrimage" to Uganda moved the people we showed it to—especially the miraculous way I had found Frankie's family. Those who knew Frankie gasped when they saw a picture of Frank—much in the same way as Frank did when he saw a picture of his brother for the first time.

People could also see from the photographs that we had been able to help some vulnerable children in Uganda and knew we wanted to continue to help in some way. A number of people asked if I had thought about setting up a charity. It seemed like a good idea, but it would also be a big commitment and I didn't know where to start.

A few months later, a friend of mine, Margaret Reid, purchased tickets to see the band Level 42 live in Glasgow on October 18, 2012. Level 42 was Frankie's favorite band; in fact, it was the last band he ever saw. It was also their song that we played at his funeral. I'd never seen the band live before and was a bit apprehensive about going as I thought I might find it too emotional. But I decided I really wanted to see them as I was sure Frankie would have wanted me to.

The night of the concert, we were right down front waiting for the band to come on. I handed Margaret the money for the tickets but she refused to take it and said, "I want you to put that to your charity in memory of Frankie." I told her I didn't have a charity set up. She smiled and said, "Well you have a donation. You had better start one."

Although I had been giving some thought to setting up a non-profit organization, I don't think it was until that night that I knew I was going to go through with it. It felt as if Frankie was right there beside me, egging me on. When the band started to play "Starchild", I found I was surprisingly okay—not reduced to the bubbling wreck I had expected. Perhaps the time was right for me to do something in his memory. Besides, Margaret had just given my "charity" a donation.

I came home from Uganda with a dream to build a school and to help the most vulnerable in Uganda. Mainly orphans. There were as many orphans in Uganda as people in Scotland! I also wanted to help girls receive an education in a culture that did not seem to value them as much as boys. And vulnerable women, to help them survive after husbands had died, beaten them, took other wives, or left them destitute. To me, empowering people and education were key, and fit perfectly into my dream to build a school in honor of Frankie and Janet. Sounds romantic, eh? I was soon to discover that, like anything worthwhile in this world, it required a tenacity, courage, and strength of will I wasn't aware I had. It also required a lot of help from a lot of other people, not least of all Rony Bridges, who apart from being my emotional rock was my entire right hand.

Well, anyone who has attempted such a thing as setting up a charity from scratch will know that it is not easy. The only easy part was picking the name—

Starchild. One day I found myself sitting in the middle of the floor, surrounded by the application forms for charitable status. I was finding it so complicated that I was ready to rip it all up and give in to apathy. In my sheer frustration, I posted a status on Facebook saying I was tearing my hair out trying to fill in the paperwork required to set up a charity. Two minutes later—I am not exaggerating—I got a private message from an old school friend, Lynn Campbell, who knew both Frankie and me. She told me she understood the kind of forms I was up against as she dealt with them at work and offered to help me. I couldn't believe it! It seemed the universe was giving me exactly what I required, exactly when I required it.

Then on February 14, 2013—Valentine's Day—I received an email headed *SCIO Award*. Lynn and I had done it! Starchild had been granted charitable status by the Office of the Scottish Charity Regulator (OSCR).

I was overwhelmed with joy! One thing I know for sure—I could not have done it without Lynn's gracious help and that of some very close friends who had agreed to become board trustees. Lynn later told me she had never experienced an application going through so quickly and without any further questions asked.

Now, my primary concern was to get people to believe in the project as much as I did, and for them to have faith in my ability to carry things forward. To my surprise that part wasn't as difficult as I had thought. The hardest thing was having faith in myself and believing I could see this through to fruition. My heart was full of good intention, but I was a realist. I knew there were pitfalls when dealing with Uganda; the corruption and bureaucratic red tape there were a well-documented nightmare. I was also cripplingly aware of the do-good tourists and aid workers who come to Uganda with a white savior complex. I might have grown up with a Ugandan black brother and had deeply personal reasons for wanting to help but I was as naïve about Uganda as some of the people and organizations I was criticizing. There was no doubt there was a gulf between myself and those I wanted to reach out to. I was scared. I didn't want to invest other people's hard-earned money and get it wrong and I didn't want to work in Uganda and end up making things worse because of white ignorance. How on earth was I going to navigate it all?

The Taboo Challenge

As a new charity, we knew we had to garner public confidence in Starchild before we could take on anything really ambitious. It's hard to tell people you are going to build a school in Uganda when you haven't proved you can complete *any* kind of project out there. We knew people would need to see some evidence that we could work with the locals and change lives before they would take us seriously. What Starchild needed to do was to tackle some small, manageable projects that we could share on social media to build support for our school plans.

When my new brother, David, first asked me to visit his government school in West Kulungo, Masaka, I was surprised at the high ratio of boys to girls. David told me, sadly, for many African girls, education is a considerable challenge. Patriarchal structures are still deeply embedded— especially in rural life. With limited funds, the boy child is favored when it comes to education. Most often, the girls are forced to marry as early as thirteen years old and don't have a chance of secondary education. I discovered that Uganda has one of the highest rates of child marriage in the world. And, once a girl has her first period, she is considered ready for marriage. A young bride whose honor has been protected can fetch a good price. For poor rural families, it is understandable why marriage can be an attractive option. Going to school can be a risky business, with many girls becoming victims of rape—often on the way to and from school. Girls also learn from an early age that sexual favors can be bartered for almost anything, including rides to and from school. With many having to walk up to five miles a day—hungry and thirsty— you can imagine the exploitation that can happen. Domestic abuse is also rife in many families. It is, therefore, most often thought better to marry girls off early rather than run the risk of their girl child losing their honor within the family or elsewhere.

And, for those lucky enough to get a chance of an education, something as natural as menstruation can mean an end to their education.

David explained most families could not afford any form of the necessary sanitary protection, so by the age of puberty most girls are forced to drop out of school. He also told me about the huge stigma surrounding menstruation in Africa. Many males think it is dirty and that girls are cursed. They are often teased so badly that they stay away from school during their monthly cycle. Many are even ostracized in the community.

I had heard about this being a huge problem in Third World countries but it wasn't until I spoke to some of the girls at David's school that I grasped just how appalling the situation is in Uganda. Many of the girls told me how they missed important exams, having to stay at home and sit in the sand instead for almost a week. Many resort to leaves or rags, which is *not* sustainable throughout the school day. Unsurprisingly, this can lead to embarrassment and worse, infections. I also witnessed a distinct lack of sanitation facilities and almost no hygiene care, which makes managing menstruation an absolute nightmare for these girls!

My heart went out to them. No girl *anywhere* in the world should be stigmatized, forced to miss school, or have to drop out because of something as natural as their menstrual cycle. When I shared some of their personal stories with the Starchild board, we all agreed to take up the challenge and try to help these girls. The social problems we knew would be much harder to tackle and with limited experience, the last thing we wanted to do was bulldoze our way into a country with our "Western" conditioning without fully understanding the background to the social conditionings in Uganda. Besides, until we proved we could follow through with concrete projects, build some trust in Uganda and at home, we had no hope of challenging some of the social injustices. If we could at least provide the girls with sanitary care we would be helping to empower them.

Rony has a very creative brain and let's just say he is also in touch with his feminine side. Quick as a flash, he came up with what I thought was a brilliant campaign. We called it *The Taboo Challenge*. The idea was that men would go into a chemist, pharmacist, or supermarket, buy a packet of sanitary products and take a selfie holding the box. When they did, they would post the picture on Facebook and text 'taboo' to Starchild, donating £3. They would then nominate a male friend to do the same. Well, I guess if you are going to do something, it might as well be controversial. After all, they do say there's no such thing as bad press.

Much to our delight, most men joined in and shared the challenge with one another—those who didn't were shamed into making a donation anyway. It was the cause of much hilarity as some men treated a pack of tampons like Kryptonite in the hands of Superman! After the initial few videos and pictures—some by local celebrities—it took off amongst our Facebook friends and we raised enough cash to buy every girl in the school sanitary care for a year. But perhaps the biggest thing that came out of it was that some male teachers in David's school in Uganda also took selfies holding packets of sanitary products and posted them on Facebook. This was unprecedented! We had not only broken a bit of a taboo in Scotland, but we had broken a huge taboo in Uganda.

It wasn't long before we discovered another *very* large charity, whose name I won't mention, was hijacking our idea. Rony and I had been trying to promote the campaign nationally and had written to Channel Four News, the Lorraine Kelly Show, Tampax, etc. to help boost awareness of the campaign but, sadly, to no avail. Suddenly, less than two months after we launched our campaign, this large charity—with a lot of Who's Who on their board—took our idea and ran with it. They somehow managed to receive *plenty* of media attention. Oh, well, at least some more girls in Africa benefited from it. But it still would have been nice if they had acknowledged the creator behind the campaign and given Starchild the visibility boost we so desperately needed. No one on our board was getting paid, let alone a six-figure salary. Go figure.

Comfort and Joy

Uganda

The day starts out well—we are even at the equator bang on time. We've brought friends to Uganda for the first time. Helen is an arts workshop facilitator and Iain is the treasurer of Starchild. Iain and Helen get to witness the water going down the hole clockwise on the north and anticlockwise on the south side—just like I did during my first visit to Uganda.

Frank, me, David and our driver stopped to pose at the equator

As it's one of the main tourist attractions, Iain buys his first Ugandan football top and Helen manages to find a few gifts from the crowd of vendors. We take our time shopping and even grab a spot of lunch. I have already warned my muzungu friends that no matter where they eat it is best to be cautious, but there's a small restaurant to sit down in and everyone is hungry. I must be getting braver as I decide to order a Rolex—No, it's not a watch—it's a chapatti wrapped around egg, usually along with some onion and tomato.

Phibi's husband, Pastor Sam, has come along to help today. I'm grateful as he drives a people carrier which has enabled us to bring more MakaPads on this trip. It must have been a tough job filling his vehicle because Pastor Sam has ordered mounds of matoke! Or, perhaps it's because he's wearing a dog collar and he's getting special treatment?

Thank goodness we do eat because a few miles up the road our second vehicle in the convoy —carrying Pastor Sam, my brother David, and many boxes of sanitary products—breaks down.

After receiving their distress call, we make our way back and find them at the side of the road. After the third boda boda driver comes past and slows down to eye up the muzungus, I decide it is not safe for us to stay here. We are carrying three cameras, mobile phones, iPads and a reasonable amount of cash; we are sitting ducks.

David hops on with a boda boda driver to get help in the town. Once he has arrived back with someone from a local garage, we hightail it out of there.

Rony claims David is sixteen stone after he climbs in the front of the pickup, practically sitting on top of him. Sadly, we have to leave Pastor Sam behind. At least he is wearing his dog collar. It is doubtful anyone will bother a pastor with a bunch of sanitary products in his van.

We have already passed a road block on the way here; we know we can't go back through the same road block overloaded with passengers like this, or those lovely traffic "angels" might do more than fine us.

Instead, David takes us on a detour. He tells us it will take twenty minutes. Ugandans tell you what you want to hear—it could be a two-hour detour for all I know. At least Helen and Iain will get to see village life up close. Then Rony asks to stop the truck. I assume that perhaps his sandwich back at the equator isn't agreeing with him, but no, he has decided that sitting on boxes of sanitary pads on the back of the truck would be much more comfortable than sitting squashed up with David.

Soon we have a convoy of children chasing after us, waving to the mad muzungu who is sitting like a cowboy on top of the vehicle. Rony distributes as much pocket change as he has, and the children run after the truck as far as they can.

An hour and a half in, it's my turn to stop the truck. I have to have a "short call" as the Ugandans so charmingly call it. There is no pit latrine around here so David gets the driver to pull the car up outside someone's home. I ask if he knows the owners and David shrugs his shoulders—Ugandans love to do that when they can't or won't answer. I am mortified. Thankfully there is no answer at the front door. I go around the back in search of the latrine but once I see it, there is no way I am going in there! I'd rather pick a bush! I'm learning to squat quite well, so I pick my spot. David doesn't want to leave me, so he hangs around not far from my spot. I've been holding on so long that I produce a river that immediately runs right past my brother. Oh, the joys of Uganda! I'm just thankful that no one on today's trip has had a dodgy tummy. We've ALL suffered in that way at some time or another.

David assures us that it's not far now. Do I believe him? Of course not. He's lost. Nothing is signposted. He stops a few boda boda drivers along the way. I'm getting nervous again as I've seen the same driver, wearing red, appear then disappear, then appear again. I imagine the worst—there's going to be a convoy of boda boda drivers around the next winding road and we are going to be held up at machete point.

Just as I am starting to panic, David spies the first school we are visiting—St. Francis. We are now two and a half hours late, but no one here is bothered. Despite the fact they have been standing in the heat for hours waiting, the children greet us with the usual Ugandan flare: busuutis blazing across the grass, hips swinging, tongues trilling, and drums beating. The fact that we have just survived an arduous drive through the heat and along the dusty, bumpy road doesn't matter; all is forgotten. Who could be anything other than happy listening to these children?

As Helen and I produce the sanitary products, Iain sheepishly takes his leave and decides to check out the structure of the buildings.

There is soon much giggling and hilarity as Helen pulls out her pink Marks & Spencer panties and I demonstrate how to use a MakaPad.

MakaPads were invented by Dr. Moses Kizza Musaazi at Makerere University. They provide low-cost, effective protection. They are made from papyrus and paper waste. The fibers are beaten, dried and softened using no electricity. They are also ninety-five percent biodegradable, which is extremely important given Uganda's sewage problems.

I have learned things in Uganda I never knew about sanitary protection. It was incredible to hear from the pioneers who designed this product and to discover the research that was done to ensure a low-cost alternative to keep girls in schools. But these senior primary schoolgirls aren't interested in the details of how they are made; they are just so thrilled to see hundreds of packets of them. They will no longer have to worry about missing school and exams. It might not seem like much, but these sanitary products will transform their lives right now and their opportunities in the future.

We are running late for our next visit, but I've been asked to plant a tree at this school in honor of today's events. I find it pertinent as the school is called St. Francis. Frankie's name on his birth certificate was Francis. The last time I planted a tree, it was in his memory, at Pollok Country Park in Glasgow. His ashes are scattered under that tree.

Our next school is Kubungo Secondary School—David's school. Fortunately, it is only a few kilometers away. We are so late arriving that the school day is actually over. The children should be off collecting water for the family, however, much to our delight, all the students and teachers have waited for us.

We unload the truck as quickly as possible while the students organize their dancing and singing to welcome us. A short ceremony later and Helen and I are ready to distribute the sanitary products. I am concerned we can't give each girl her full supply as Pastor Sam has the rest in his van and it has been hours since we last heard from him.

Just as we start to hand out what we have, our prayers are answered; Pastor Sam appears and saves the day! We can give each girl in the school her supply for the next six months. The other six months we give to one of the female teachers. Each month through the term the girls will be given the rest as required, signing for them each time. If we give them all out now then we run the risk that other female family members will take the girls' pads from them, or they could even be persuaded to sell them.

Next, we are off to the science department, my brother David's department. The first time I was here I witnessed David teach. I was impressed with his teaching, but I knew he was struggling to teach science with only one microscope for a class of thirty or so children.

On our first trip to Uganda we met two lovely chaps, Graham and Mal, who were working with a Christian organization called Tools with a Mission. They worked with TWAM to refurbish old or discarded equipment of all kinds: sewing machines, microscopes, tools, and farming equipment. When we met, they were also in Uganda for the first time, visiting some of TWAM's projects sites' and showing the communities how to use the tools. They happened to be staying in the room next to us at the guest house.

It was Mal's birthday while they were there and I suggested we go out for a meal to celebrate. I will never forget Graham's face. I was sitting talking to him when he turned white and pointed behind me—I was scared to turn around as I thought someone had a gun at my head. That was the night we saw the circus of rats running around the open-plan kitchen and we had just eaten! There's nothing like an incident like that to bond you for life. Once I started Starchild, Graham told me if I ever needed anything to let them know and he would try to help me.

Well, our charity needed microscopes. I had called Graham and he immediately offered to start collecting any that came his way. In less than a year we had been able to provide forty microscopes (and some prepared slides) for David's class.

Today the children from David's science class are lined up with their microscopes and slides to demonstrate with enthusiasm the difference this equipment is making to their education. I hope to use this experience as a starting point for organizing a science bridge project with Dr. Mhairi Stewart from the University of St. Andrews in Scotland that empowers Ugandan girls to become scientists. It's an exciting project that will focus classroom discussions on health-related topics in Uganda. In particular, we hope to raise awareness and understanding of the prevalent diseases that communities face on a daily basis such as malaria, typhoid, HIV, TB, and sleeping sickness. The fact that we now have these teaching tools in place will really help, and I'm delighted to see the profound benefit the microscopes are already having.

It's been a long journey to Kabungo Secondary School, but completely worth the effort. As we drive off, we are astonished to see the girls from the school carrying their six-month supply of sanitary products on their heads. It's endearing and emotional to see them showing off with pride something that is usually so taboo. They may not be aware, but it shows solidarity with the fight women have for equality. I drive off full of hope that these young women might one day empower other women in their country to fulfill their potential and transform their lives. We are all responsible for helping marginalized women in countries around the world. It is essential to help free them from poverty and brutality and give them dignity and purpose.

Jelly Beans and Gin

It has been a long day and everyone is tired and hungry; before we head back to Kampala we need to eat. David suggests a restaurant we may like, inside a local hotel. As we drive up the exotic pathway to this impressive building Iain whispers in my ear, "I suppose we muzungus will be footing the bill again. Why not pick the best place in town, eh?"

It's true: the muzungu always gets handed the bill and it can be disheartening. Even the wealthy Ugandans expect us to pick up the tab. However, as a deputy head teacher, David would have to pay a third of his weekly salary for one meal here. I know that David is trying to be thoughtful by taking us here; he wants to show us a beautiful place to eat in his town. The hotel is grand, with that old-world British charm that still exists in parts of Uganda. David tells me he was hoping we could have come here earlier in the day in order to see the beautiful gardens too.

As we walk through the large glass doors we become aware that we are the only people there. There doesn't even seem to be any staff around. My first port of call in a Uganda establishment such as this is always to look for the ladies room and today is no exception. After walking the vast, lonely corridors I find myself a VIP loo. Hurray! But I'm brought instantly back down to earth by the substantial array of free condoms on offer and the signs decorating the walls warning me about sexually transmitted diseases. I surmise the hotel has a reputation for casual encounters of the intimate kind. Suddenly I don't feel like sitting on the loo after all and practice my squatting skills yet again.

On my return I find our group already seated at a long table by the window. I'm glad to see Assis, our driver, is sitting alongside everyone without me having to request him. Normally drivers sit at a separate table for dinner, but I don't like this custom. We are surrounded by elegant tables but still no people. A member of staff has been found in my absence and Rony informs me a round of drinks has been ordered.

Soon a large African gin and tonic is put down in front of me. Ah, just what I need after a day like today. "Cheers everyone."

A beautiful African girl approaches our table and asks if we are ready to order food. Ready? We're all starving! The menu looks great. David has picked a lovely place. It's just bizarre that there are no people here. By the time everyone has ordered their food, my gin is done and Helen and I are asked if we would like another double.

Forty minutes later there is no sign of food—not even smells coming from the kitchen. I smell a rat, well not literally, but something doesn't seem right. David decides to go in search of another member of staff. He comes back shortly and tells us the food is on its way, and that they had to wake up the chef.

"Wake up the chef?" I look quizzically at David.

"Yes, Sister. You see, I did not know the restaurant is usually closed on a Monday. But it is not a problem, Sister. Not a problem at all. They are happy to oblige. The chef is now awake."

Thank goodness for small mercies. I assume the chef stays in one of the rooms here and this isn't as big an issue as it sounds. Iain asks me why they didn't just tell us that when we came in. Is it not evident to him yet? We are the walking wallets—the muzungus. Of course, they don't want to turn us away.

Another gin and another half an hour later we are still waiting, and there are still no smells of food. This time it is Pastor Sam who decides to see what is going on in the kitchen. A few minutes later Sam returns and tells us it won't be long now as the chef has arrived from the village. Since Ugandans tell you what you want to hear, the chef might as well be in Timbuktu. As I sip my third—or is it my fourth?—gin, I overhear a potential political nightmare playing out at our table. There has clearly been too much drink and not enough food. I know only too well that politics, religion and drink shouldn't be mixed. Add in cultural naiveté and we could be asking for trouble. Assis excuses himself and goes in search of the chef. I sense he has deliberately removed himself and has probably gone to pray —for food I hope.

Finally, food smells start to drift across the table and smiles appear on our drawn faces. But not for long. Assis is back from prayers and is the first to almost yelp when he puts his fork into the fish, which is practically still frozen. It's not long before everyone is complaining the food isn't properly cooked. By this point Iain's face is red with rage. Rony speaks to him in local Glaswegian slang, "Keep yer heid, big man." Translated, it means "Maintain your composure my friend." However, our dear friend, Iain, is way beyond composing himself. He stands up and starts ranting and raving about this total farce, attempting to instruct the ever-increasing number of staff around us about how to increase tourism in Uganda. Oh dear, his blood sugar levels must really have dropped. Suddenly there is a manager, deputy manager, porters, cleaners—everyone has gathered for the fascinating spectacle of an angry muzungu. Now, we have been informed on numerous occasions to never lose our tempers with Ugandans as they treat it as a sign of immaturity. While Iain has his meltdown, Rony quietly negotiates the bill and we hightail it to the car. A few minutes later Iain is followed out by a polite entourage of staff attempting to pacify him. His parting message to the manager is a Glaswegian saying, "Get on yer bike!" To which the manager calmly replies, "I'm sorry sir, I don't have a bike."

As Iain finally gets into the car, I ask Helen if she has *any* food in her bag. Peanuts—anything. Helen opens her handbag and says, "I have some jelly beans. Anyone want one?"

CHAPTER EIGHT
Wishing Upon a Star

By the end of Starchild's first year, people were starting to give their time, talents and money. As a result, we were able to organize some charitable events, enabling us to fulfill some good projects in Uganda. We used the power of social media and the facilities of local churches and clubs to show what we had achieved. Not only had we provided a year's supply of sanitary products to the schoolgirls, but we also delivered over eight hundred mosquito nets to schools and clinics, provided school tables and chairs, scholastic materials, school uniforms, shoes, clothes and much-needed supplies to children's homes. All of these worthwhile activities garnered public confidence in Starchild. As a new charity, we not only had to build trust with our supporters, but I had to create a sense of confidence amongst our board and inspire them to trust in me and my vision. We were serious about building a school. Were it all to go wrong, I would not only feel terrible for letting down people in Uganda, but my reputation as a person of integrity in my own country could face ruin.

If Starchild was going to build a school, the first thing we needed was land. But there was a major sticking point; as muzungus we couldn't legally purchase land. And even if we did, it might not be worth the paper on which it was written. I already knew through Moses' experience that buying land in Uganda was unreliable—even some Ugandans don't know if they legally own the land they are building on or already live on.

We had heard many horror stories of charities losing millions through corrupt dealing. We witnessed projects that had been started by charities who had later walked away because of the corruption. Some people we met had naively sent money across to Uganda and expected a school, church or orphanage to be built—with no supervision.

I recall one man telling us his church back home in the United States had been donating money to a local pastor to build an orphanage. The church was regularly sent pictures of the construction and heart-warming photos of orphans. Eventually, this man from the States decided he had better go out and see this orphanage for himself. Wisely, he decided to arrive unannounced. It turned out there was no orphanage. The only construction being done was an extension to the pastor's home!

Another man told us his church back in the States had been supporting a 'church' in Uganda for over a year, with a congregation who were supposedly doing God's good work and transforming the lives of Uganda's most vulnerable. Now, to be classed as a *real* church, it had to have a congregation of at least sixty. Again, this man from the States got a tad suspicious and decided to take an unannounced trip to Uganda.

When he arrived, he phoned the pastor and told him he was coming to visit the church that Sunday. The church turned out to be nothing but a shed, with exactly sixty people crammed into it. Some of the attendees had Bibles in their hands, but these were mainly being held upside down. It didn't take him long to figure out that the congregation was made up of some local villagers who had been paid a few shillings to turn up for his visit.

By this point, I had witnessed lots of projects that were started all over Uganda with the best of intentions and then sadly left to ruin. The Ugandan hand is often out for 'chai' as it is called. Little can get done without a backhander, even in the banks. Few seem to do much without thinking of lining their own pockets. It's destroying the country, the charities, and the good people who are trying to help. But most of all it is hurting Uganda and those good citizens who find themselves embroiled in a corrupt system.

I arranged many meetings during my next trip to Uganda. However, most were with time-wasting bureaucrats who didn't like dealing with a woman—especially a muzungu—and worse, one who refused to pay chai. It soon became evident that the best thing for Starchild would be to partner with a reputable organization or school that already existed and was in need of financial support.

As muzungus, if we were seen as the front people for the school then we would be paying extortionate costs for everything and wouldn't be able to get anything done unless we continuously paid chai. That would mean that every day obstacles could be put in our way. Even getting the school registered could be a potential nightmare; it would most certainly involve a large bribe for someone to pull strings. Most of the schools in Uganda are at the mercy of this game. Even with the best schools, it usually takes at least three years to become legally registered, and the threat that a school could be closed at some bureaucrat's whim is always there. We remained undeterred, but realistic.

Back in Scotland, Starchild was lucky enough to have a respected architect, Gary Mochrie, the brother of one of my dear trustees, Lisa Trainer, donating his time and talents. Gary brought the Starchild vision to life on paper. I remember how I cried with joy when he first gave me the plans, beautifully bound in a folder. As fate would have it, Gary asked to meet with us to hand them over in what used to be the old Greek Taverna, now known as The Mulberry Street. Unbeknownst to Gary, it had been Frankie's old watering hole—and mine, until I left for Canada.

The vision seemed more real now I had something tangible to show people. Then Gavin Coley of Abacus Modelmakers, who had been our next-door neighbor and Frankie's friend, agreed to build a model of the school from Gary's plans. Such generosity of spirit was truly humbling.

Much to our sadness, we then discovered that the plans couldn't be accepted in Uganda unless they had been produced by a Ugandan architect—at least that is what I was told. I wonder if some *chai* might have helped. It was one of my first *very* painful lessons. Starchild always knew our plans had to stay fluid, but this setback proved just how difficult the red tape in Uganda could be. Perhaps I was wishing upon a star that I could pull this project off.

Fortunately, no egos got terribly ruffled, but it was a huge disappointment for everyone involved. The fact remained that we had professional architectural plans and a fantastic model of our concept to show people, both here and in Uganda. This gave us credibility; it was hard not to be impressed with the Starchild vision when you looked at what Gary had created on paper and Gavin had brought into a different dimension as a model.

It was time to go back to Uganda.

The Sins of the Father

Uganda 2015

Today I am meeting with Leonard Okello from the Uhuru Institute for Social Development in Kampala. Our friend, Moses has told me Leonard could potentially offer Starchild some advice about the dos and don'ts of setting up a not-for-profit organization in Uganda.

Rony, Moses, and I walk up metal stairs to the small office tucked away inside a larger building. The door to the office is open and Leonard's voice welcomes us in. Immediately, another man, who is sitting at the table facing us, stands up and says, "Moses, my friend! It is so good to see you. I didn't expect to see you here. This is wonderful. Just wonderful."

I am struck by this man. His height, his presence, everything about him is striking. He hugs Moses, who practically disappears in his arms. He then turns his attention to Rony and me. He shakes my hand warmly and puts his other hand on my shoulder. His hands are huge! He is huge!

"I'm Jaffar, Jaffar Amin. It's lovely to meet you."

The name Amin jumps out for obvious reasons, though I assume it is a common name in Uganda. But I can't take my eyes off this guy. He's stunning! High chiseled cheek bones, slim African nose, intense eyes and broad shoulders. His smile is as Hollywood as his presence.

He tells us he had just popped in to see Leonard and doesn't want to intrude. Moses insists he sits down and has a coffee with us; Leonard has already put on the kettle. Jaffar tells Rony and me it has been years since they last saw each other and hopes we don't mind him joining us for a bit.

Of course, we don't. I'm quite taken by his charm and good looks. Jaffar goes on to tell us how much Moses means to him. He explains our friend, Moses, helped him at a time when he was trying to come to terms with his name. He said Moses helped him own up to his name and prayed with him at a time he needed it the most. Since then, Jaffar says, he has been on a mission to reconcile with the many victims of his father's tyranny.

I can hardly believe it—this must be Idi Amin's son! I can only imagine the presence his father must have had if this is his son. I feel a shiver.

Moses explains to Jaffar we are here to see Leonard about our charity, Starchild. He offers him some background about the charity and why it was set up.

Jaffar engages deeply in the conversation about Starchild. His face and body are animated as he listens to Frankie's story. Then he reaches his long arms across the table to me. His fingers are long and slender, his palms almost white. He cups my hand in his, puts his other hand on top and looks right at me. "It's been so *lovely* to meet you today and see my old friend, Moses. It's such a beautiful coincidence that you had a meeting today with Leonard. Starchild sounds wonderful. Helping other people is so important. Like you, I am dedicating my life to helping people."

The energy from his hands is magnetic.

Jaffar goes on to tell us he feels that being Idi Amin's son is like carrying the weight of a million tons on his head. But forgiveness, he urges, is the only way forward. "Though difficult, we cannot continue to wallow in bitterness in this country."

He recalls to us how he turned up at a village one day to give a talk about reconciliation and a woman ran out from the crowd. "She ran straight for me and started beating my chest again and again. I allowed her to hit me as hard as she could. I just stood there until she could hit me no more. Eventually, she crumbled before me in deep sobs. I bent down and put my arms around her and wept with her and asked for her forgiveness for my father and my family."

I'm just about weeping listening to him. This is surreal. Here I am, sitting across from Idi Amin's son. I have been entirely saturated in the history of his father and the atrocities of his brutal dictatorship for the past several years while writing my novel. And now I'm in Uganda listening to his third son tell me about his life with him as a father.

"My father called me over one day and said, 'I have a sweetie for you, Son. Open your mouth and close your eyes.' My father put a chili in my mouth and held it closed. I could hear him laughing as I was trying to scream." Jaffar chuckles like a giant. "I think he was trying to toughen me up. That is one of my earliest memories of my father."

I see the sadness in the story and the sadness in Jaffar. Despite his honor, he is wounded—deeply.

Then he says, "I am Muslim, but we are all one in God. Would you mind if I lead us all in prayer?" Jaffar holds out both his hands. "Let us form a circle of prayer."

We all hold hands and bow our heads. Even his voice is captivating. With my eyes closed, I could be listening to a BBC news presenter. He prays for Starchild, he prays for peace, for reconciliation and truth. He thanks God for bringing old and new friends together today.

His prayer is sincere and warm. I want to believe this man is a good man who truly does want to be a vehicle for healing and forgiveness in a country that is still reeling from its violent history. A history that Jaffar feels has at times been manipulated by the media and not truly reflective of his father. He disputes some of the histories of his father as an insane tyrant and tells us he is, in fact, writing a book to set his father's record straight.

I tell him I can't believe I am sitting with him today. I am honest and tell him I don't think he would like the depiction of his father in my book. I say to him I have read a lot about his father in the context of Ugandan history.

He is humble and understands why I would choose to portrait his father negatively. He feels there is perhaps a greater reason we have been brought together today and offers an exchange of emails—he wants to share his writing with me.

Uganda is still to this day a fiercely patriarchal society. Its tough warrior exterior could do with some softening. Perhaps Jaffar can show Ugandans that there can be a different kind of warrior. Perhaps. But it is too early for history to tell.

The Mango Tree School and Learning Centre

Nankwanga Village
Malindi, Jinja,
Uganda

Today we are on a mission to deliver another two hundred new school uniforms to The Mango Tree School. Our alarm clocks are set for 6:00 a.m. as we have a long journey ahead to Jinja. It might look close on a map, but the Jinja road is one of the busiest in Uganda. Although it is a single tarmac carriageway road, it is a major route for large commercial vehicles. This can mean vehicles speed and overtake dangerously. Accidents are as frequent as the roadside traders of snacks. The Mango Tree School is in Jinja, approximately eighty-three kilometers from Kampala. Jinja sits along the northern shores of Lake Victoria, near the much-contested site of 'the source of the Nile', a small spot along the shoreline of the mighty river.

Delivering new uniforms to The Mango Tree School

Jessica Norrby runs the school. Jessica was a child soldier in Museveni's army during Uganda's raging civil war. She was one of the lucky survivors who found refuge in the UK. On my first visit to Uganda, I tried to find a child soldier to interview for my book but I didn't have much luck. Then a British chap, Eric Walford, I met out here suggested that I interview a friend of his, Jessica, who lives in London.

The first time I spoke to Jessica was on Skype. Much to my surprise, she openly shared her experiences with me. It was painful for her to recall, but I was grateful for her willingness to let a total stranger into that dark period of her life. The stories I chose to tell of child soldiers in my novel are not representative of Jessica's story, but it was important to hear her journey. It was also the start of a deep and lasting friendship. Against the odds, Jessica has risen in life. She is proof that it is the resilience of the human spirit that wins. She is passionate and committed to helping needy women and children in her country.

Jessica told me she owned some land near the Nile in Jinja and had built a mud hut school there for vulnerable children. She asked if we would visit it while we were in Uganda. I was more than happy to agree, not just to see her school but because the journey would take us over the Nalubaale Dam, the primary source of electricity generated from the water of the White Nile. I couldn't believe I was going to get to witness the white plumes of water.

During Idi Amin's rule the dam was often blocked by human remains—leftovers from the crocodiles. Some say, they were the only ones who benefited under his rule. Today, beautiful white egrets elegantly balance themselves on the water hyacinths. These purple, free-floating plants are the only ones now trapped below the dam.

The Mango Tree School sits in the most beautiful location imaginable. Set back a few hundred yards from the lush, evergreen riverbanks of the Nile; the area surrounding it attracts both a vast array of bird life and a lot of tourists. However, most of the community living near this bank are as poor as they come.

The school is free and so is mainly filled with orphaned and impoverished children. Many are refugees. They are offered one meal a day at The Mango Tree School. Often it is the only meal these kids will receive in a day—hence some walk up to seven kilometers to come here. That and, of course, a free education.

The first time Rony and I visited the school was in 2012. Back then there were sixty children, one notepad and two pencils. We asked them what they needed the most and they all said, "A school uniform—please!" So for Christmas that year—Starchild's first year as a charity—we set up a Christmas uniform campaign and managed to buy them all uniforms. Can you imagine giving a child in the Western world a school uniform for Christmas? But that was what they wanted and so that is what we gave them, along with the dignity and respect a uniform commands in Uganda. One little girl wrote to me, "Thank you. My uniform makes me shine like gold."

Since then the school has grown to house over 216 students, and Starchild continues to buy their uniforms, some school materials and sponsors those transitioning from primary to secondary school.

Today we are picking up the new uniforms en route to The Mango Tree School. I have been praying for the rain to hold off; the clouds have been like a womb about to break water for days now. I feel bad praying that the rains hold off as Uganda has just suffered a bit of a drought. However, it is now April, smack dab in the middle of the rainy season and I know from experience that the smattering of rainfall we have experienced this morning could change rapidly into a monsoon.

Despite the recent drought, the land is still looking lush. Beautiful land filled with tea, sugar, and coffee plantations embrace us most of the way. Before Idi Amin expelled the Asian community of Uganda in 1972, Jinja was a thriving city with elegant colonial-style homes and plantations. That legacy is still evident today. However, much has been left to deteriorate and is in need of restoration.

It's not long before the foreboding clouds seem to hug us as well as the plantations. The skies open up just as we reach the local tailor to collect the uniforms. The scene erupts into a powerful storm that Zeus himself would have been proud to create. The downpour causes the roads to become dangerous. I know it will be impossible for our people carrier to make it through the thick, red murram mud which paves the way to the school. Our only hope is to walk. I happen to have spied a pair of Wellington boots in the back of the vehicle. Although they are three sizes too big for me, I make a dive to grab them first!

This mud is a nightmare to walk in, like trying to walk in butter. The build-up on my boots soon makes me feel ten feet tall, but by then I can't move and have to be levered out of the mud by a local man with a big stick. Rony opts to roll up his trousers and walk in his bare feet—but he gets stuck too and another friendly local has to help pull him out of the mire.

Usually we are greeted warmly, with children waving flowers and singing. But today the children are huddled inside, peering through the small entrance of their primitive classrooms, waving frantically at us while protecting themselves from the rain. A few brave souls venture out to welcome us, fueled by sheer excitement.

The school is the most ramshackle building you can imagine, but that is its charm. It's a flagship to this struggling community, one that has built itself a school with the materials they have on hand: murram mud, cow dung, and wooden sticks.

We are taken through each classroom and greeted by the teachers and classes with singing, praise, and letters of thanks. It's all very moving and at times I feel tearful listening to the precious letters of thanks they have written for us. It's truly humbling.

Just as on previous visits, we are told by most of the pupils they want to be a doctor, lawyer, teacher, pastor, engineer, or a pilot. All the school children we have visited so far in Uganda have those same high ambitions. I can't get over the dichotomy—in Scotland if you asked a bunch of school children what they wanted to be many would say a movie star, a musician, or an artist. Creativity doesn't seem to be encouraged in the schools we visit in Uganda.

I ask a teacher about one of the children who is not doing so well at the school and she says, "Oh, I think he is just stupid."

I quickly say, "How do you know that child is stupid? How do you know that if you put a paintbrush in his hand, he wouldn't become the greatest painter in Uganda?"

She tells me she never thought of that before. She then tells me it is a waste of time to think that way as there is no money for pencils, let alone paintbrushes, and it is better not to give the child a false sense of hope.

What chance do these children have when, as far as I can tell, most of the Ugandan education system is only interested in producing academic children? Frankly, who can blame them? For some families, sending a child to school is their only hope—these children are under enormous pressure to succeed. They often become the lifeline to their struggling families. I can understand why there is no money available for paintbrushes, musical instruments and sewing machines, but my heart goes out to the children struggling with the three Rs: reading, writing, and arithmetic. I know that pain myself.

When I was at school in Scotland, back in the seventies, children who were not very academically inclined were often pushed aside. I remember only too well being teased by a teacher for not being able to spell and not being "clever"—yes, dear Mrs. Edminston. The name used to haunt me. I spent many years feeling anger toward her and believing she didn't deserve to be a teacher. Her teasing was nothing short of cruel.

I empathize deeply with the children who are not faring so well here in Uganda. I was anything but academic at school. I wasn't good at the three Rs, but put me in a class that included drama, music, art, or sewing and I was not only happy but often excelled. God only knows where my self-esteem would have been without access to the arts.

It is becoming evident that most of the children I meet in Uganda will never get that same opportunity to discover their creative talents.

Giving children Art Packs at
Mango Tree School and Learning Centre

The old feeling of isolation from my schooldays grips me. I was scared to go to school because I mostly felt out of my depth. At exam time I often became sick. Our education system has now changed and recognizes that not all children learn in the same way or at the same pace. And, of course, dyslexia is now widely recognized. But this is not yet the case in Uganda. Neither do they seem to recognize autism, Asperger's or dyspraxia. In fact, I'm starting to realize that Ugandan children with these conditions are most often hidden away and the families shamed. People here believe it is a curse that has befallen the family—particularly the mother and child.

It sounds like something out of our history books. Even two nieces of the late Queen Mother were hidden away from public view because they had learning difficulties. Thankfully the West has moved on and learned to recognize these conditions for what they are, and children with these challenges are now given opportunities to express themselves.

I drive away from The Mango Tree School feeling unusually depressed—but not by the immense poverty. It's closer to home. A nerve has been hit. It's the old buried emotions of Mrs. Edminston surfacing. I thought I had dealt with them!

I wish the gatekeepers of education in Uganda could open the gates wider and accept the diversity of teaching styles and of students' needs. I wish they could ensure that all the children have a chance to fulfill their potential, and fully recognize that in *every* child there is a star.

Finding the Star in Every Child

My plans to build a regular school were morphing into a belief that Starchild should *really* build a school specifically for the creative arts. Art, in all its forms, is not only educational and entertaining but above all inspirational; it can heal wounds and promote understanding and peace.

The arts is where my passions and talents lie, and those of Rony's too, as an actor. Most of our friends are artists from all walks of life and I felt sure we could get at least *some* of them to support us. But it would mean a shift in direction for the charity and I wasn't sure how our board and our current supporters would feel.

I knew we had to remain open and not be rigidly attached to our ideas, but it suddenly seemed that perhaps I had been leading myself in this direction all my life. Perhaps the season was right for the dream of a school for the creative arts to manifest.

Art class at the Starchild School for Creative Arts

Much to my delight, the Starchild board understood my change of heart and were only too eager to get behind the concept. The Starchild board had also begun to realize that building a school for the creative arts meant we wouldn't have to embroil ourselves in the unrelenting red tape of the official education system. The subjects we wanted to teach were not in the school curriculum; therefore, Starchild would not be at the mercy and scrutiny of an often-harsh education board.

Soon we were attracting support and interest from artists all over the world. Facebook was a great tool; our artist friends started to share our dream of a school for the creative arts with their networks. They understood the power of the creative arts to communicate, inspire and heal. Much to Starchild's delight, they not only spread the word about our project but also started to offer us their own art to sell. Rony had one of his brainwaves and came up with the concept of *Art for Africa*. With the help of the artistic community far and wide, Brian Clements of McTears Auctioneers in Glasgow, and Starchild's lean, thrifty operational style, we achieved our fundraising target needed in order to start building our school in less than two years. However, we still had to address the issues of where to build and with whom to partner.

A Date to Remember

Uganda

There is something quite thrilling about being led through a no-go area in Uganda. It's certainly an adrenaline rush. I am forewarned of the dangers of the market by a member of the hotel staff, "Muzungu lady, you are *insane* to go there—my brother will go for you. Tell me what you want. We will get it for you."

And I am sure they would, but I want to experience this place myself. Besides, I have my brother David with me and Rony, too. I am also becoming aware that Ugandans often exaggerate the dangers of their own country to muzungus. I haven't quite figured out why, but some would have you believe that there is danger lurking around every corner. I sometimes think I have more faith in the inherent goodness of their countrymen than they have.

The reason we are here is that we were told we can buy mosquito nets for £1 rather than £4 on the high street. It is a dangerous market—particularly for muzungus—but we reckon it will be worth it if we can indeed buy more nets for the kids with the money we have raised.

David holds my hand tightly as we navigate the labyrinth of narrow streets. They are filled with vendors and shoppers, everyone pulsing along to blaring beats—although the real *funk* of the market is fouling my nostrils. I feel like a human pinball as I ricochet against hundreds of dark, sweaty bodies, all pushing and pressing up against me. I swear some of the men are deliberately using the tight confinement as an excuse to touch me up. Rony is slightly ahead of us and can't see this. I'm glad as he would most likely hit someone and then we really would be in trouble.

I watch in wonder as local women tote large baskets of goods on their heads, somehow managing to weave their way gracefully through the skyscrapers of pots and pans. Buckets and basins threaten to fall over like the Leaning Tower of Pisa. My senses are on overload.

David has already been on a scouting mission and promises me he has found the best mosquito nets money can buy—all at the best price. I know David's previous market scouting missions for me haven't always worked out exactly as planned—remember the floral arrangement? But let's face it, just how difficult can it be to pick out a mosquito net?

I am so wrong about this, and more than a little overwhelmed. There are thin ones, thick ones, single ones, double ones, portable ones, romantic ones, square ones, round ones, floral ones, pink ones, blue ones, frilly lacy ones, treated ones, non-treated ones, long lasting, lifetime guaranteed ones!

This Asian vendor thinks he has won the lottery: a muzungu lady is here to buy four hundred mosquito nets! He's a sweet talker and I get the full *bhoona* of a sales pitch laid on for me. By the time he finishes explaining the *vast* differences in mosquito nets, I am exhausted and in need of a cold drink. I only have to say the word and a tray of drinks arrives before me. Of course, I have to pay for it and everyone else's, including the vendor's.

In the end the deal is done over a cold Fanta. Four men are employed to carry our large bags of nets to the van parked at the opposite edge of the market. I'm pleased to see that it's not just women who have mastered the art of head-loading. Our head porters maneuver swiftly through the jam-packed market, carrying an absurd load of mosquito nets on their heads.

Our driver, Lucca, has never been so happy to see us! He tells us he has been waiting nervously for us to return. I love our driver. He has the kindest of natures and is a real gentleman. He is so warm and friendly toward us. He is from Moyo, in the north of Uganda. Moses' hometown is Moyo and he has known Lucca since he was a boy.

Lucca's work has been cut out for him, driving us around—we're all already exhausted. Rony, Moses and I have had two weeks in Uganda this time, with the pressure of finding the right project to partner with. We have already visited three potential projects and delivered numerous amounts of practical materials along the way, but there is still one more project to visit.

My phone rings.

"Michaela, it is Phibi. My dear, I am so sorry we have not been in touch sooner. I cannot believe you have been in Kampala for almost two weeks and we have not yet seen you. Can you visit our school on the twenty-sixth, my dear—that is this Thursday—when Pastor Sam will be here? Can you come then, please?"

The first thing that hits me is the date. February 26 is already indelibly printed in my memory because it is the anniversary of Frankie's death.

Since I have last seen Phibi and her husband, Pastor Sam, they have built a primary school in Vvumba. I have not yet seen the school but I have been sent regular updates of its progress. I know Phibi and Sam very much hope that Starchild will partner with them—as do *all* the projects we have visited.

Grace Primary and Nursery School is situated about forty kilometers north of Kampala, in the district of Luweero. It is not far from Gayaza High School where my pilgrimage began. Vvumba is also the place where Frankie's grandmother still lives.

On the last few miles of our drive to the village, dense plants, and small Bantu huts surround us. This is real village life. A few stray goats and chickens slow us down but no one is in a hurry out here. Basins of washing are balanced on teenage heads while they carry a sister or brother on each hip. They meander slowly home, barefoot on the dusty red earth.

The welcome party is now in sight. Phibi and Sam are waving from the porch of their home. Their smiles are warm and friendly, as is the dog that has run to greet us.

I peel myself out of the back seat. Today is hot! The murram dust clings to the air and the back of my throat. Phibi and Sam are livelier than I have ever seen them. Our visit has caused great excitement for sure. Children peer through the open doors and windows of the school, giggling and waving at us with obvious delight.

We wave back, but a teacher soon dampens their ardor and the children scurry back to their schooling.

Phibi and Sam are keen to show us the progress they have made with their school. Construction is still underway and building materials and workmen are everywhere on the site. There are no windows or doors but the school is already being utilized. Health and safety back home would have shut it down in two minutes, but the rules are different out here.

The fact that the school is still being constructed means we can see very clearly what kind of job is being done. I'm no expert, but it all looks very professional. I also happen to think it looks a *tad* like Gary's architectural plans, which I showed them last year. I say nothing. I am happy that some of his ideas might have rubbed off, but I'm also angry at the bureaucracy I faced then, which had cast such a damp shadow on our excitement at the time.

Moses, Rony, and I visit *every* classroom and talk to the children and their teachers. The children are *very* well behaved. Most children in Uganda are disciplined, but this is a level of discipline that I haven't witnessed before and it makes me uncomfortable. I am not enjoying this school as much as I had hoped. I want the children to loosen up and not to treat us so much like school inspectors. I am uncomfortable with the formality.

But then, as if the universe hears me, the bell rings for the lunch break and I am just about run over with the zeal of these children trying to touch me. With great fervor they stroke, poke and prod me from every angle—all with boisterous hilarity. It's pretty overwhelming standing here in the middle of fifty-plus black children who want to touch me and hug me, just to say they have touched a white woman. They are fascinated by the red color of my hair and how white and freckly my skin is. One girl puts her finger in her mouth, wets it and tries to rub my freckles off. Another keeps stroking my hair—I think she is fascinated by how soft it is. I just stand there and allow myself to be examined like some kind of exotic creature. I feel like pinching myself at the irony of it all. It was always Frankie who caused this kind of fascination wherever he went in Scotland. I wonder what Mum would think if she could see the role reversal today.

Pastor Sam waves over at me and, much to my surprise, doesn't try to stop them. He stands there in his black Wellington boots, laughing away as the children practically knock me to the ground by climbing on and over me. I peer between the rioting bodies to try and see Rony. He looks like he has been trying to take pictures but now has at least ten kids hanging onto him. He gives up, turns the camera around and shows them pictures of themselves. That's when they finally leave me alone; everyone wants to see themselves in a picture! Thank God for digital cameras.

Lunch is ready. This time I eat the *fresh* chicken. I am slowly starting to get used to the Ugandan food, although to be honest, I am not very taken with it. It lacks the spices that I love so much. It is also very high in starch. Baked, boiled or steamed matoke comes with every meal, as does sweet potato and cassava. Today I am grateful there are no grasshoppers to be seen—they are considered *quite* the delicacy.

Over lunch, much to our surprise, Phibi and Sam offer us some of their land to build our school for the creative arts. They admit the concept of such a school is alien to them but say they are willing to learn. They believe it will complement their own school and be a first of its kind. There are many children at Grace School and in the local community who could benefit from such a school. But we are well aware that Phibi and Sam will benefit too.

We stroll to Grandma Miriam's house—she only lives about three hundred yards away from the school. As we walk the dry road I think about Frankie's ancestral footprints. His mother must have walked on this land. I feel as if the murram road holds footprints of all those who have walked its winding path.

When we reach Miriam's home I imagine Frankie has been there waiting for me. I imagine he bends down before me and rakes his hands through the red murram dust, picking some up. He holds out his dust-filled hands to me. I take some of it in my own hands.

I wish it were magical dust—like fairy dust. I wish I could be transported back in time to visit Frankie's ancestors. I know his spirit has been here and he has now seen his lineage. He's at peace.

Miriam is so happy to see us. She is dressed in her busuuti and is tongue trilling with excitement. I sit on the couch beside her and we hug and hug and hug. I tell Miriam it is the anniversary of Frankie's death today. Phibi says she had no idea it was an anniversary when she suggested we come to Vvumba today. Miriam throws her hands up in the air in prayer position and praises the Lord with such passion! She believes God has brought us together for a reason. We must pray.

Pastor Sam leads us in a prayer dedicated to Frankie. The intensity of it is touching. Miriam keeps saying *Amen, Amen.* I choke back tears.

When Frankie died, if anyone had told me I would one day be sitting in his grandmother's house in Uganda on the anniversary of his death, saying prayers with a pastor and some of his relatives, I wouldn't have believed it possible.

Arts for Africa

It became apparent during—and after—our last trip to Uganda that the school we should partner with was Grace Primary. The board made that decision because Phibi and Sam proved that they could project manage the building of a school, work with the education authorities, and were in an area of need, not because they were tangentially related to Frankie. Also, Hope Kollective, the children's home we visited on a previous trip to Uganda, was within walking distance from Grace Primary. We knew that if anyone was in desperate need of access to a school like ours it was the impoverished children from Hope Kollective.

Sam, as a pastor, was held in high regard by the local community and without community support, nothing can be achieved in Uganda. Both he and Phibi had drive and ambition—both of which were needed in huge quantities for a project like ours. Sam also has an entrepreneurial spirit; he was eager and willing to learn. He also had a vested interest in the success of our school because it would be linked to his own. He had already proven to us that he could get things done and done well.

After months of lawyers, due diligence reports and lots of phone calls and emails, a memorandum of understanding was drafted up between Pastor Sam Lwere, his wife Phibi, Grace Primary and Nursery School and Starchild. I won't bore you with the details of the tedious hours of work it took to get to an agreement, but let's just say we kept our wits about us and developed good negotiating skills through some pretty creative accounting—never accept the first, second or even third costing of anything in Uganda.

In July 2015, Starchild broke ground on Phibi and Sam's land in the village of Kakoni, Vvumba, Uganda, and started construction of The Starchild School for Creative Arts.

While the school was being built, we needed to get set to work to provide the teaching materials necessary for it to function as a haven for creativity. We needed art supplies, sewing machines, musical instruments, fabrics, threads and craft materials.

My first call was to Graham Hart at TWAM. Much to my surprise, Graham told me they already had at least eight sewing machines sitting at their warehouse in Ipswich that they could ship over to Uganda in their next container for us. I couldn't believe it—just like that, we had our sewing machines.

Music and sewing at the Starchild School for Creative Arts

I then put a message out on Facebook asking if anyone had any discarded musical instruments lurking in a cupboard or under the bed. I was overwhelmed with the response. In less than two days, we were offered umpteen guitars and violins, a professional drum kit, a couple of trumpets, flutes, and tambourines; the only thing missing was keyboards. I put out another call on

Facebook specifically looking for keyboards and by the end of that day I had four!

It was incredible, but how on earth were we going to get them to Uganda? I knew TWAM was great at navigating the red tape in countries like Uganda, and its shipments always got there without anything being tampered with, but I wasn't sure if it would be able to help us ship our goods.

Graham suggested we email David White at TWAM and ask if it was at all possible to book some space on a container and we would pay for it. Again, much to our surprise, David, said yes! It turned out Graham had been following the Starchild projects on Facebook and was able to tell him that any goods sent on our behalf would be employed wisely. By now, we had repeatedly proven we could navigate Uganda. I was so pleased we had taken the time and effort to build our reputation before trying to launch our school.

Next, I put a call out for unused art supplies on Facebook. Our original *Art for Africa* auction had been a great success (preparations were well underway for a second) and in the process we had garnered many artist friends online. In no time at all, we found ourselves inundated with an array of fantastic art materials. Thanks to Helen McVey and a charity in Glasgow she worked for called IMPACT Arts, a vast array of donated art and craft materials were able to go in our container.

As I knew the owner of Remnant Kings fabric shops in Glasgow, I decided to ask him if he would kindly consider donating some fabric for the kids to use as practice. To my surprise, Farrell McKeon told me I could go to his warehouse and uplift a thousand meters of fabric!

What had at first seemed overwhelming turned out to be one of the easiest parts of this remarkable journey. Still, our donations had to be collected from all over Scotland, packaged up and made ready for a driver to take to Ipswich in July. From there they were put in a container and shipped to Uganda. Somehow, we managed it and within a few months, we had a large container chock full of goodies ready to be shipped to our school, even though it still wasn't fully built.

How we managed all this, I will never know. You see, on May 22, 2015, just a few months after we returned from Uganda, Rony was diagnosed with lung cancer. We were told he had months to live.

CHAPTER NINE
Uganda Saves a Life

Uganda, 2015

It is a hot day, our last in Uganda. We are invited to a garden party at the Sheraton Hotel for the Kampala School of Music. Fred Musoke, a prominent musician in Uganda, owns the school. Serendipitously, I was introduced to his British wife, Sam, through the actress Sally Philips. Rony happened to have a part in a movie, *Decoy Bride*, that Sally had both written and starred in and I was lucky enough to meet her on set. She was just lovely, and when she heard I was traveling to Uganda, she contacted her friend Sam and we also became friends.

It is a gorgeous day at the Sheraton in every way possible. The wine is flowing and David, Moses, Sam and her children and some other friends are with us. We are celebrating the end of an exhausting trip.

Suddenly—and unusually for him—Rony says he isn't feeling well and thinks he should go back to the hotel. Reluctantly, I leave the party with him. We have a long trip home the next day and Rony seems really tired, but I put it down to the grueling pace we are under, and the heat.

A few days after we return home, Rony still doesn't seem very good. He is tired, with hot sweats, and a constant cough. By this point he has had this cough for a while, and I had been nagging him to go and see about it. This time I insist he go to the doctor's in case he has contracted malaria. He argues that we have both been taking our antimalarials, but we also both know they can't guarantee immunity. Reluctantly, Rony goes to see his GP, Ian Kennedy.

Ian isn't taking any chances and admits him to Gartnavel Hospital right away where they have The Brownlee Centre for Infectious Diseases.

Well, they don't find malaria—they find cancer. Lung cancer. They also discover Rony has contracted community-based pneumonia and that is the most likely cause of his symptoms.

In a matter of months our world has come crashing down. A series of tests show that the lymph nodes seem to be involved, which means the worst. They say ignorance is bliss, but I am anything but ignorant when it comes to cancer. I nursed Mum through ovarian cancer and fully understand the prognosis. If we are lucky, my Rony has a few months left on this earth.

I don't want to dwell on the enormity of the grief and anguish we are both feeling. There are already plenty of books written about the devastation of a diagnosis such as we have been given. I say *we* because there are two people who have been given the diagnosis. Two people are fighting to keep body and mind together for themselves and each other.

Apart from the initial trauma of thinking I am going to lose the man I love, I am devastated that after all this time and effort, Rony won't live to see the school in Uganda. Without him, I doubt there would have been a school. How can life be so cruel? But I know it is that cruel. Bad things happen to good people. I've known that all my life.

I do the only thing I can—I pray and I ask for prayers all over the world. I contact everyone and anyone I can think of. I ask for healing, for Reiki and for candle lighting. Anything. I'm not praying for a miracle. I am merely praying for the strength for us both to get through this.

The PET scan shows the lymph nodes in the center of the chest are "lighting up" and appear crushed—a sign they have cancer. However, the biopsies of the lymph nodes come back clear. After six *very* uncomfortable bronchoscopes, the medics decide to surgically remove one of the lymph nodes by doing a mediastinoscopy and send it for analysis. Much to the medical team's surprise it comes back benign. It seems even though it looked to this team of professionals like the cancer was in the lymph nodes, it wasn't. No one is able to understand this. We are told it is an unusual case, but the evidence from the biopsy shows clearly that the cancer is contained in the lung.

This means Rony has a chance! There is the potential to operate and remove the tumor and part—if not all—of the infected lung. But he still has pneumonia; despite umpteen antibiotics it won't shift. It is getting to the stage where the surgeon, Mr. Butler, knows the tumor has to come out or it will be too late.

Eventually, after the strongest dose of antibiotics they can give has been administered, a decision is made. They have managed to bring his white blood cell count down enough to chance the surgery.

I will never forget the day Mr. Butler tells Rony he will be having the operation in the next few weeks.

Rony says, "I'm sorry but I can't. I'm in the middle of our big *Art for Africa* auction. People are relying on me."

Mr. Butler looks straight at me, then Rony, and says in his thick Irish accent, "Well, let me tell you something

Mr. Bridges. If you don't have this operation right now, you might not be here to see *Art for Africa* in a few months."

On September 1, 2015 Rony undergoes surgery to remove a section of his lung. From his hospital bed in The Jubilee Hospital we handwrite, together, the catalog for *Art for Africa*. Rony refuses to change the date of the event. He makes it his goal to be fit enough to be at the preview reception with the artists on September 18. And he is.

Despite a few errors in the catalog, *Art for Africa* is a huge success and we raise over £24,000. Subsequently, Rony undergoes radiotherapy. Six months later, Rony is fit enough to return to Uganda.

A lot of people think—and tell us—we are mad to go back to Uganda after such an ordeal. But as far as we are concerned it is Uganda that saved Rony's life. If I hadn't thought there was a strong chance he had malaria then Rony wouldn't have gone to see his GP, and Ian wouldn't have rushed him to hospital and the cancer wouldn't have been found until it was too late. So, you see, we have reason to thank Uganda.

A Dream Comes True

Uganda, May 2016

I walk along the red murram dust floor of our school, disappointed that it is not concreted. We had, after all, sent the funds for this to be done. I ask why our school does not yet have a proper floor. Pastor Sam looks up, "Ah, yes, the floor is on the ceiling."

That is when Sam informs us an official had turned up and told him that because we have music in the school, we needed an acoustic ceiling. I'm not sure who we were going to annoy with the sound of music—perhaps a herd of elephants?

Apart from this surprise diversion of funds, we have managed to build a rock-solid 180 square meter school for £16,000 as against quotes of £100,000. And it will be finished on time!

Celebrations outside the newly built
Starchild School for Creative Arts

In August 2015, just prior to Rony's surgery, our shipment of equipment arrived at the school. Seeing the photographs of the joy-filled children and teachers receiving these gifts made the hard work involved in getting them there worthwhile.

I know having both the school and *Art for Africa* to focus on has helped us get through Rony's illness. When faced with a prognosis like Rony's, some people put their slippers on, feel vulnerable, and stay home rather cocooned. It's not unusual to feel fragile and afraid to continue participating in life to the same extent. But for Rony and me it was important to try to have as normal a life as possible. Of course, despite a desire to do so, he was not physically able to do what he did before. Although he didn't have the same energy levels and was battling deep seated fears about his mortality, he was determined to push through the emotional and physical pain and engage in life as much as possible. As his partner, I was fighting my fear and anguish of losing him. I was also learning to be less mollycoddling and allow him to do things, even when I was anxious that they would be too much for him. Again, some well-meaning friends suggested we both slow down, but for Rony and me nothing propelled us more than the feeling that time could be taken away from us. We had to make the absolute most of every day! Also, I truly believe knowing that we are helping others, helps *us* in so many ways.

Our treasurer, Iain Andrews, turned out to be fantastic at helping us work out the exchange rates and in dealing with a lot of the financial practicalities. Iain is an old school friend of Frankie's, and I have always seen it as a lovely twist of fate that he ended up being our treasurer. And, of course, our friend, Moses Apiliga, has helped enormously with the legal preparations and negotiations in Uganda. Lisa Trainer of Red Door Interiors donated all the furniture to our school, and it looks spectacular. All in all, Starchild is blessed with a great team of people without whom our dream of this school wouldn't have stood a chance. And now there is just one week to go until the school is officially opened.

My heart beats as fast as the loud African drums I can hear from a mile or so in the distance. I see Grace Primary first, then the children, all lined up to greet us, dancing in their grass skirts. I take a sharp intake of breath. I cannot cry. *Wow, wow, wow*, I say to myself. *This is for real. We did it!*

I feel like royalty as we step out of our vehicle. A procession of children and teachers dance, sing and tongue trill before us as we walk, shimmy, and clap through the Ugandan pomp and ceremony on the red carpet of murram dust.

My thoughts are on the other side, with Frankie, Janet, and my parents. I imagine that they, too, are here waiting on us. I imagine Frankie and his great big smile, waving at me from the top of the steps. "Would you just look at this place, Sister—it's jumpin'!"

As we reach the top of the procession, I feel like the Queen trying to shake hands with every child and every teacher. Then I let go of the pomp and ceremony and start to dance along with the kids. I don't care if I am making a fool of myself with my strange, white-lady moves; I'm happy—overjoyed, in fact! Everyone is, especially when I try to dance. The kids giggle but manage not to lose any momentum in the performance they are putting on for us.

I see the large sign outside, STARCHILD SCHOOL FOR CREATIVE ARTS. All the artists and people who supported us—we did it! We built this amazing school!

After a long prayer and dedication by the local pastor, Pastor Lawrence, I am taken by surprise when I'm asked to unveil a plaque on the wall dedicated to Frankie and to Starchild. I can no longer hold back the tears as Pastor Lawrence motions me to pull back the blue curtain and unveil a beautiful bronze plaque. Then I'm asked to cut the ribbon, which has the design of the Scottish Saltire Cross on it (Okay, I brought that with me.) The tongue trilling reaches a feverish height as I cut the ribbon and allow everyone in—all six hundred of them, including local dignitaries.

I am led through the large door by Pastor Sam along with Rony and my new Ugandan family. My brothers, David and Frank, are right beside me. The large partition walls have been pulled to the side and chairs for hundreds of people have been set up on either side. The children have painted pictures of Frankie and they are displayed all over the walls. Silver stars hang from the ceiling—the ceiling that should have been the floor, but all has been forgiven. Grandma Miriam has been waiting down at the front for me, sitting proudly in the new wheelchair that Starchild has bought her. She is elated.

Music, singing and drumming fill the air as ancient tribal celebration dances are performed for us until everyone is almost giddy. Many people take turns trying to teach Rony and me some of the dances. The children find great delight watching our futile muzungu attempts to keep up with the rhythm.

This is the kind of welcome and thanksgiving that keeps bringing me back to Uganda, that encourages me to keep going, despite the enormous challenges this country provides. This is what it is all about. Despite the immense poverty, there is such immense joyfulness. A joyfulness the likes of which I have never experienced anywhere else. And yes, neediness. A neediness that I and Starchild have somehow, miraculously, been able to help with. We did it. We built this incredible school and these children in front of us right now are learning the arts and thriving.

We are shown the art class, the music class, and the sewing class. The children demonstrate what they have learned and perform for us. It is a hub of activity. I can hardly believe the scene before my eyes. I am joyful and so is Rony, because there is simply no better feeling in the whole world than to know you have been able to help in some small way, to make a difference for even one person.

The Starchild School today

I stand alone outside for a moment, listening to the cacophony of sound coming from inside the school. I thank God for this day and I thank God that Rony is here with me and still in remission. It is one of those moments where I just breathe and think—we did it. I listen to the heartbeat of the school. Strong. Young. In its infancy. It will be here well after I am gone. I pray it will nurture thousands of children and give them an opportunity to learn the creative arts. I don't think until this moment I realized just how monumental this project really is and the impact it will have on the lives of those who are lucky enough to come through its doors. I thank God once again for giving me the gift of Frankie as my brother. I will never understand why he was taken from us so soon, but I know his legacy is well and truly living on in a continent he never knew, with a family he never knew. The whole thing is just miraculous.

A Christmas Present

A few days before Christmas 2016, I decided to clear out my Facebook Messenger—something I rarely do. Much to my surprise, I discovered some messages that, for one reason or another, I hadn't opened. I get a lot of personal requests from Uganda for help, and I have to ignore most of them. Unless I know the person or there is a mutual connection, I tend not to open the message. However, on this occasion I opened a message from a stranger, Christy Hill Puckett. I discovered she had actually sent it to me the previous year!

Much to my surprise, this stranger told me a friend of hers had randomly come across a video on YouTube of Rony and me with her son. She wanted to let me know she had adopted Lawrence, the little boy whose operation we had paid for on our first trip to Uganda. I was overwhelmed: what a great Christmas present!

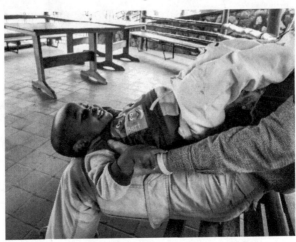

Rony playing with Lawrence after his surgery

It was just fantastic to find out what had happened to Lawrence after all this time. Christy told me she lived in the States, in Mississippi, with her husband and two other children, a boy and a girl. She attached some beautiful pictures of them all together. Since then Christy and I have become friends on Facebook, and it's always a joy when I get updates on Lawrence and his siblings.

While I was in Italy, taking some time out to finish writing this book, I decided to message Christy and ask if she would be willing to speak to me about her experience of adopting a child from Uganda. She said she would be happy to talk to me about it. I imagined I might chat with her for around twenty minutes or something, but we spoke for over two hours. Thank God we have free mobile phone calls on Messenger now!

Before that call, I had doubts about this book and of telling some of the uncomfortable truths about Frankie and the adoption. I had asked Frankie to give me a sign that he was okay with me talking about him and, of course, my parents too. After that conversation with Christy, I was convinced I had to finish writing this book. You see, Christy was facing the same challenges with multi-cultural adoption that our family had faced. She spoke candidly about some of the daily issues they were having, and her fears for the future. She told me she wanted me to finish writing this book, that there was a definite need for it. Talking to Christy was a bit like talking to my mum. Some of her wounds were much the same, and so were Lawrence's. I hung up, knowing in my heart I had to share my story.

A Letter from America

Dear Michaela,

I've just finished reading your book and I am completely in awe. Thank you. Thank you. Thank you! People say that life is full of coincidences, but I truly believe it's just God using people as vessels and in this case, it's you, Rony, and, of course, Frankie.

Abandonment and post-adoptive trauma is something that no one really talks about, so I thank you for sharing your mother's feelings, and your own. You have been able to draw on your experience as a daughter, a sister and wife of adoptees.

You see, of all of the children in the world, Marty and I both knew that Lawrence was our son the very moment we met him. There is no way to describe it other than to say it was as if they'd handed me a baby I'd just birthed myself. We KNEW he was our son. He just happened to have been born to another woman on the other side of the world. And he just happened to be black. He also had a coconut-sized hernia that needed repair, but we were prohibited from sending money to the orphanage in case it was seen as trafficking because we so wanted to adopt Lawrence.

We later learned he had also suffered a severe tongue infection and chronic, untreated, upper respiratory issues. We prayed continuously for healing for Lawrence (now called LP—this was HIS decision) and hoped that someone would care for him.

I emailed the babies' home every few weeks to see how he was feeling. It is no coincidence to me that you and Rony 'just happened' to show up and pay for the very life-saving surgery that he needed and then cared for him as he sat in that dirty sandbox after that surgery. To me, that answered prayer started with Frankie. If it wasn't for him, there's a good chance Starchild would have never been born. If Starchild had never been formed, Lawrence may not be alive today. And if he were, it would probably be under very different cir-cumstances, so I hope you and Rony both understand the magnitude of my gratitude to you both.

From the outside looking in, I feel like God had far greater plans for Frankie than anyone could have ever known. Frankie may have only been grant-ed twenty-seven years on earth, but because of him, hundreds of Ugan-dan children have now been cared for. Thank you for allowing his life to be shared through your writing.

Many children now have a future that they otherwise would not have been able to access. I'm speaking freely here, but in America, we say "the good die young" and Frankie was good. Although I will never meet him, his short life on earth has had a long-term impact on many children, including my own son, and that irony is not lost on me. Frankie may have been abandoned as a Ugandan in Scotland, but Frankie's life has had a profound impact around the world.

Uganda is a beautiful country, full of life and joy in the simplest of things, but it is no place for an orphan to live. There is no free education, no healthcare, and no government programs to ensure that they are fed. Yes, there are some selfless, warm souls who are good and kind and honest, but the nation as a whole seems to be corrupt. As you point out in your book, it is a difficult country to navigate, but it's so culturally rich that it's worth the trouble. Children without families often find themselves in remand homes (a.k.a. child prisons). I can name exactly four that we've visited first hand and I still struggle with the things I witnessed six years ago. It is enough to make you wish you could adopt all of the children that resided in these homes, but that in itself creates an even bigger problem: "adoption tourism."

Adoption tourism is something that I, myself, am guilty of even though it was not done intentionally. Because so many people are now adopting from Uganda and neighboring African countries, it has become a very lucrative industry. I can say with one hundred percent honesty that our adoption was done as ethically as we knew how, but we met other muzungus who admitted to paying "expediting fees" for visas and passports. But that is another story for another day.

Like Frankie, Lawrence will never know his biological family. Lawrence was abandoned outside of a hospital in the Kololo region of Kampala, near the embassy buildings. We don't have any details other than he was "between one and two years of age, he was very sick, and that he was dressed in a green jumper." When he was found on the bench, he'd been crying, "Father, Father." My heart can't even take typing those words. Lawrence has scar tissue on his vocal chords from all of his screaming and crying when he was young. It hurts me to know that those cries probably went unanswered. He has asthma and scarring in his lungs from chronic, untreated upper respiratory infections and pneumonia. He has burn scars down his forearm that we cannot explain and he underwent $26,000.00 (USD) worth of *dental surgery when he came to America because his gums and teeth were so damaged, due to both neglect and tribal tooth extraction.*

Lawrence is so loved, but he also struggles with the subconscious reminders of abandonment. He bonded to me and his sister, Brogan, very quickly. It helps that Brogan has the patience of Job and is very motherly and attentive. However, it has taken him years to form an attachment with my husband and our other son, Swaid. Despite this, I' am the one who gets the brunt of his defiance. He adores me and will tell you that I'm his "favorite," but he loves to push my buttons and test the limits of my patience. He needs me and he wants me as his mother, but he's quick to see what he can get away with. I think it is his subconscious desire to know that my love is unconditional. Marty and I regularly tell him, "Mommy and Daddy love you. We will always be proud of you. And we will never leave you." This verbal reassurance has helped tremendously with his attachments, but he'll require long-term therapy for his Post Traumatic Stress Disorder and other disorders stemming from his early childhood and subsequent neglect.

You have verbalized some of what I could not express. Although it's difficult to deal with, I find comfort in knowing that I am not alone. Everyone hears about the happy stories of the orphan that finally gets a family, but no one is prepared to talk about the often harsher reality of it. Adoption stems from loss and no one really understands how powerful that is unless they've walked through it. Adopting a child of a different race is a whole other issue. We've been fortunate that trans-racial adoption is becoming more common in Mississippi, but racism will always be evident and stupid people will always ask stupid questions. (I'm looking at you, super market cashier! And yes. I AM his REAL mother.)

I'm getting side tracked now, but it feels so good to be able to talk about Lawrence and the circumstances surrounding his story with someone who truly understands. Thank you for listening to me ramble, and thank you for your honesty in this book. Lawrence has a long way to go for healing, but he's getting there. That would not be possible if it weren't for you honoring Frankie. Your story is so deep and so moving that I almost cannot grasp the reality of it. Finding your brother's family in Uganda and the coincidences surrounding that was nothing short of a miracle. As the mother of an orphan, I thank you for sharing your story. As the mother

*of Lawrence Agaba-Mukisa Puckett, I
thank you for saving his life.*

*All my love
-cp
Christy Hill Puckett*

The Magic in the Universe

The net of events that have brought me to this moment
make me realize life is not as wild or as random as most
people think. There is a refined, divine intelligence to it.
I believe I have genuinely glimpsed the unfathomable
genius of it all. I know I have experienced the magic in
the universe.

The random chance of Christy's friend finding me
on YouTube and us being led to each other proves to
me yet again just how crazy and wild synchronicity in
life can be. Sometimes when these bizarre things happen to us it challenges the status quo. People can start
to think it's odd or *I'm* weird. Believe me, at first I felt a
bit perturbed by it all. But I was also curious and therefore open to it.

Now I wake up feeling more like a child does, willing to let the universe, God, or whatever one wants
to call it, lead the way. I don't have the same need to
control things in my life. I know the divine intelligence
is one step ahead, planning it all in its own miraculous
way. Some people might say things like this don't happen to them. They never used to happen to me either,
but since I've been open to it, the synchronicities have
kept coming. I've also learned to trust my inner wisdom
much more. It's also beautiful and powerful to believe in
the radical spontaneity of life. When ideas come, sud-

den impulses and opportunities, I don't dismiss them—they might be divine nudges. I'm aware being open to movement and growth is supported in life, stagnating is not. But *we* have a choice. Being unwilling to break-out of our molds or merely responding to the molds of those around us does our true self no justice. I love days of radical aliveness, having a thought and acting on it in the moment can be so liberating. And, the more one recognizes blessings, even the tiny ones, the more blessings seem to come.

Some people questioned my sanity when I told them I was going to build a school in Uganda, but I felt I was becoming saner than ever before. I was more awake and willing to take a leap of faith. That's not to say I was impractical and had my head in the clouds. The challenges, as you've read, were real, as were some of my fears. No one waved a magic wand and did it for me. Just like writing my books.

This journey has taught me to love myself more. I have also learned to embrace a bit of the rebel in me when dealing with the challenges in Uganda, and dis-covered I could become a bad ass when it was needed. And yes, I pissed some people off—mainly the men in Uganda.

There will always be people out there who will want to shoot another person's dreams down and can't feel happy for others when they should. It's probably be-cause they are not following their own dreams. But I was delightfully determined, and knew I had Frankie and the magic in the universe with me, as I pursued my dreams.

Life is never the same after death. The loss is ir-reversible, final and terrifying. The grief of never, ever seeing someone we love again is *absolute agony*. Our natural human response is to cling to what has ended.

Death can become a dead weight. Eventually I was faced with a choice. Allow the weight to drag me down, or release the fear, believe in the impossible and reconnect with my passions. In so doing, I not only free myself, I free my loved ones. Frankie and I gave each other life after death.

Some people laugh when I tell them I talk to you, Frankie. But I can't imagine not doing so. I wonder how you feel now seeing your school and everything that is being done in your memory. Can you believe all this! Would you have ever imagined there would be a charity named after you and so many children would be learning the arts, painting, playing music, and making things with their hands? I bet you're laughing right now because you weren't good with your hands. I'm smiling because you liked artsy things, and you did try, but let's be honest, creativity was not your strong point. I won out in that department—although, you were pretty good on the trumpet but you had no patience to learn it. Football—that was your love, and being outdoors, running, and riding your bike. I couldn't ride a bike. Remember when I fell off one at Grans. I was so black and blue! That was the last time I ever sat on a bike, but not you. You'd go for miles and miles. Uncle Jack was reminiscing recently and told me you arrived at their door one day in Cambuslang. He said you had biked it there on your own. That must have been almost ten miles away, and you were only about ten years old. I remember you ran the Glasgow Marathon. It was your birthday that day September 22. Stephen and Linda had a wee cake for you when you crossed the finishing line. I still have the medal you won. I also have a curl of your hair. Did you see me remove it from your blanket after you died? I slept with that blanket over me for a while.

So many lives have changed because of your legacy: vulnerable women and children have been able to keep a roof over their heads by learning how to sew and work their land with arable and livestock farming. Orphaned children are being given a chance of secondary education, and marginalized groups are being given a voice and opportunities because of your life and your death. I can hardly take it all in at times. You alone know the times I've had my head in my hands and wanted to walk away from Starchild. Some days it's all been too much: the need is too great, the funds too little, and the work too hard. But I can't. So many of the children remind me of you. I reckon God must have had a bigger plan the day Mum and Dad saw you in Tanker Ha' and eventually brought you home for keeps. I can't imagine how my life would have

*been if they hadn't. I loved having you
around—even when we were fighting.
But we always had each other's backs.
I sense you still have mine. I can still
hear you pushing me on just like you
did when I was scared to go to school
and you'd tell me it would be okay. We
always stuck up for each other in the
classroom, if not at home. Remember
how we always told everyone we were
twins! After you died, a teacher wrote to
Mum and Dad and said Miss Devsi had
told her how she never forgot the way
we came into her classroom together in
primary one and told everyone we were
twins. She laughed but agreed we really
were. Oh, how you were loved! No one
who knew you has ever forgotten you.
We all love you, Starchild. That's what's
written on your plaque at your tree. The
tree we planted in your memory and
scattered your ashes under. That great
big wonderful Weeping Copper beech
tree at Pollok Country Park where you
loved to play football. I swear that tree
rules the park. It's like something out of
a Tim Burton movie. I think it comes to
life at night and wanders around the
park like it owns the joint. It's the most
unusual magical tree in that whole 360-
acre country park, but then it has you
and now Dad and Mum under it. What
else could I have ever expected it to be
but magical?*

A Rangers footballer and a Christmas angel

EPILOGUE
A Growing Legacy

Starchild believes our school for the creative arts can have a significant impact on the lives of those it touches. International artists will learn a great deal from Ugandan arts and culture, which is encouraged and promoted through our program. We are optimistic that it will attract the attention of the international community and, as a result, encourage artists from all walks of life to visit the school, participate in activities, and inspire the children.

We also hope some people might consider a scholarship fund or trust fund to help further the education of a particularly talented child who has no way of paying for further training in their subject.

Starchild has artists from all disciplines ready and willing to work with the children. We hope this network will grow quickly. On top of the experiences these artists will bring to the students in an artist residency program at the school, the artists will participate in an exchange of talents and skills in the local community with local people. They will take back to their homelands what they have learned, equipped to build cultural understanding and act as ambassadors of peace and healing through the arts.

Since opening the doors of our school, it has become apparent that the most marginalized and vulnerable, especially those with autistic spectrum disorders and physical disabilities, are still unable to access any formal or informal route of education in Uganda. It came quickly to our attention that due to misguided and inherited belief systems, individuals are still being shunned by their local communities and denied their rights because of their disabilities. The behavior of autistic children, in particular, is not understood by family members, teachers, and the community. This leads to fear and rejection.

Most women who give birth to a child with a disability are abandoned by their husbands in the belief that the woman and child are cursed. If a mother has to go to work and has no one to help, she has no choice but to tie up the child when she leaves in case they wander off or are raped. Usually they are hidden somewhere so people can't find them or even know about them. Many of these boys and girls suffer rape and ridicule on a regular basis sometimes by people in the community, sometimes by family members. It is not unusual for such children to be locked up or chained in dark rooms and left there for days, often stagnant in their own feces.

The government of Uganda does have all kinds of positive polices for the inclusion of persons with disabilities. However, Starchild has seen little evidence of these policies actually being implemented, especially for the poorer in society. The number of advocates and local charities for people with disabilities in Uganda is growing and we have partnered with some of them. We recognize that many citizens have limited access to information and the necessary training to offer assistance and sensitization for these often hidden, marginalized groups, in particular those with Autism Spectrum Disorder.

On my last visit to Uganda it became apparent that there is a need for a holistic center, particularly for these women and their children, but also for their families. They need a place where they can come together to share their fears and challenges and where their children can feel safe and valued. The misconceptions and feelings of isolation need to be addressed as a whole.

Claes, Jessica, and Rony

I have most certainly overcome my fear of head teachers and now work closely with a number of wonderful head teachers in local schools. One of those schools is Williamwood High School in Glasgow. Thanks to my dear friend, Angela Smyth, I was introduced to a unique service at this school called the Communication Support Service for Autism. Starchild has since developed close links with them. We have even made a short film with this remarkable group, *We See the World Differently*. Parents, teachers and pupils came together to talk openly about autism, the challenges, and the joys. The film was shortlisted at the Scottish Short Film Festival Awards. The pupils also produced a small book for

Starchild where they wrote about how they feel. It is our hope that these tools will help us breakdown the myths about autism. These pupils also support a child's right to secondary education in Uganda and have learned so much about what it means to be a "global citizen."

Starchild is now in the developmental stages of building a holistic sanctuary to help support families and children affected by autism and disabilities.

Our holistic sanctuary is going to be called the Sunflower Sanctuary in memory of my darling Rony Bridges who died into the next life on July 14th, 2019.

Rony loved sunflowers and children with autism.

Three weeks before Rony died, Frankie came to me in a dream and told me I would soon be planting sunflowers. He said he would be holding my hand all the way. He hugged me very tightly and told me I was going to have to be stronger than I had *ever* been in my *entire* life. I knew that Frankie was telling me I was soon to lose the love of my life.

A month after Rony died, much to my surprise, Jessica Norrby offered Starchild some land to build our dream sanctuary on the banks of the River Nile beside The Mango Tree School. I could hardly believe it. Rony and I absolutely loved it there!

We hope over time, with more funds, our sanctuary could become a dedicated center, enhancing educational, vocational and social skills for this most marginalized group. Such a center could offer effective teaching and emotional behavioral therapists. If nothing else, it could offer some hope, some joy, and a break from the environment they are in. Most of these children love arts, crafts and music.

With the right trainers we could potentially help keep families together by sensitization and breaking down the horrendous myths and stigmas. No matter the emotional, physical or mental challenges of a child, there are ways to find the star in every child and to help them to shine.

As I write this, I am planning a trip to Uganda to scatter some of Rony's ashes at the place where we plan to build the Starchild Sunflower Sanctuary in his memory. Our young Ambassador Cormac O'Hara who has autism has already gifted me sunflower seeds to plant in his memory. I was told these sunflowers would be "spectacular!" How could I expect anything else—my darling Rony most certainly was!

If this book has found its way into your hands, and you feel you would like to help us to continue the work we do in *any way*, Starchild would love to hear from you. I hope you will have a look at our website and contact us at www.starchildcharity.org

Acknowledgements

I could have never written this book without the encourage-
ment, support and love of my angel Rony Bridges. Every book
needs a spine and you were it, babe! You fed me, poured me
wine, talked, listening and read, again and again my scribbles
until I finally shaped them into this memoir. I miss you every
single second ,my beautiful angel. But I *know* you are creating
Magic in the Universe.

Lynn Campbell, there wouldn't be Starchild Charity without
you. Your support is invaluable. You are indeed my KMSB!

Esther Jamieson, for reading the earliest of drafts and offering some generous editing assistance.

Anna Ross, your *Ferrero Rocher* and wine will be forever ap-
preciated, as are you my friend.

Jessica Norrby, my soul sister on this earth! You are an inspi-
ration to this muzungu!

Helen Sedgwick, for being such a great first editor. Thank you
for believing in me as a writer and encouraging me to change
the title to Starchild. It was so obvious, I couldn't see it!

John Adcox, for suggesting I send my books to The Story
Plant. The rest is history as they say! Here's to—*following
your bliss.*

Lou Aronica, for believing my story should be heard and for your nurturing guidance.

Candace Shafer, for being the loveliest of copyeditors.

Catriona Savage, every book needs a cover and you got it *so* right!

Bob Collins, for working on the black and white photographs in this book.

Ian Rae, sadly, you crossed over before reading the final pages of Starchild but I'm indebted to you for believing I was a writer when I didn't believe it myself. Here's to a *chance* meeting in Stornoway and an impulse to meet again in Paris. Both were divine nudges for sure.

Debra Kolkka, for offering me a space in your beautiful home in Vergemoli, in the mountains of Tuscany. Casa Debbio is the place every writer should be!

Anna Graham, Venafro, Italy will be in my heart and the pages of this book forever. The energy in Venafro was a blessing after Rony's surgeries. It helped us both heal.

Christina Manca, for walking beside me as I found my feet without my beloved Rony in Uganda and especially for counting the money!

My brothers Frank, David, and Paul for embracing me as your sister.

Aneez Jaffer, for my home away from home in Kampala. You are dearly missed.

Moses Apiliga, for helping Rony and I navigate your country in the early days.

Marian McCaffrey, for your constant support of my creativity over the years.

Finally, I am indebted to the Starchild board who are more like a family. You each support the charity in your own special ways. I couldn't do it without you all. It's been a magical journey together and it's certainly not over.

And, to all my friends who accompany me on this *incredible* journey called life. There is not enough space to do you each justice, but know I appreciate you *all*.

Michaela

About the Author

Michaela Foster Marsh is an acclaimed musician with three albums to her credit whose work has appeared in television and film, including *Dawson's Creek* and *The Matthew Sheppard Story*. She has been invited to sing at the Monaco International Film Festival, the Cannes International Film Festival, and for Her Majesty, Queen Elizabeth. She is the founder and Executive Director of Starchild Charity, which works primarily with vulnerable children and women and which recently built a School for Creative Arts in Vvumba, Uganda. In 2017, she was a finalist for Scotswoman of the Year by the Evening Times and has received a Prime Minister's award for her work in Uganda. She lives in Glasgow.